The Serving Leader's Guide to Effective Meetings

Transform Your Meetings with Character, Structure, and Skill

MERLE HERR

THE SERVING LEADER'S GUIDE TO EFFECTIVE MEETINGS: TRANSFORM YOUR MEETINGS WITH CHARACTER, STRUCTURE, AND SKILL

ISBN 979-8-9858839-0-9

Printed in the United States of America

Serving Leader
31285 State Highway 27
Guys Mills, PA 16327
www.servingleader.org

Designed and printed by:
Schlabach Printers
798 State Route 93
Sugarcreek, OH 44681
www.schlabachprinters.com

Some names and details have been changed to protect the confidentiality and to provide greater clarity of the content taught in this book.

All references to "Serving Leader," "Serving Leadership" and the "5 Actions of Serving Leadership" found within this and other work done by Serving Leader are explicitly permitted and encouraged by John Stahl-Wert and the Center for Serving Leadership.

Italics in Scripture quotations are the author's emphasis.

To my business partners for the last twelve years, Doug Fuhrman and Dalen Grove. It was your courageous confrontation that set me on the journey that ultimately led to writing this guide.

Endorsements

"I love this book. We hear constant stories of companies whose culture is having every meeting start two to five minutes late. On purpose! People not getting to meetings on time is a function of bad meetings which start late, don't put important decisions first, and then run long. People don't hate meetings because meetings are inherently terrible. People hate meetings because they're poorly led and managed. It takes a leader to make meetings work, and this book will help you do it well."
MARK HORSTMAN, Author of *The Effective Manager* and co-founder of Manager Tools

"You may have sat in meetings knowing that your time could be better spent elsewhere. When a meeting consists of a salad of subjects that are diced, shredded, and rehashed with no conclusions or actions agreed upon, the result is frustration. If results are what you are looking for, look no further. In this book, Merle teaches us how to make our meetings meaningful, powerful, and profitable. Make no mistake; properly structured and executed meetings are incredibly important in communicating and running any successful organization."
BILL MULLET, Chairman of the board at ProVia

"I will never see meetings the same. Merle unpacks the tactical, practical, and spiritual truths about meetings from Scripture in a profound way that will change the way you think about meetings. This book will be added to my carefully curated list of required reading for the leaders in our family of companies."
LELAND ULRICH, CEO of Corland Partners LLC

"When you read in the opening chapter how Merle responded to a critique of his leadership as president of a company, you know the author has humbly learned in the school of hard knocks. *The Serving Leader's Guide to Effective Meetings* is packed with practical guidance that is too often sacrificed on the altars of expediency and hubris."
NORWOOD SHANK, Manager of curriculum development at Christian Light Publications

"This book is a comprehensive guide to meetings written by an author with meeting experience in multiple organizations and companies. It covers the theory of what makes a good meeting and gives practical guidance to planning and conducting a good meeting. I am confident that you will find it to be helpful."
MERLE BURKHOLDER, Staff pastor of Open Hands

"Only after reading The Serving Leader's Guide to Effective Meetings did I grasp how its concepts and methods could transform a business and help it succeed. Developed by life experiences and informed by scriptural values, this guide contains tools and strategies that not only improve the quality of meetings but also strengthen teamwork, develop interpersonal relationships, and perfect a leader's serve!"
GARY PAUL MILLER, Business, church, and nonprofit leader

"All leaders should strive to be good leaders. All good leaders will strive to become great leaders. The one thing that all great leaders have in common is the ability to lead great meetings. Inversely, most weak leaders also lead boring and bad meetings. This book comes straight from Merle's heart: prefaced with compelling theory, loaded with structure and practical guides, then brought to life with stories and personal experiences. This is a must-read for every leader. The youngest to most seasoned leader will find something in these pages to challenge the person, bring clarity to the structure, and energy to the practice of their next meeting."
PHILIP HORST, Administrator of the Anabaptist Business Association

"With personal reflection and humility, Merle deeply explores the values and tenets of business servant leadership through the power of relational business meetings. Following the directives and strategies of this writing will build business par excellence while empowering individuals to develop and flourish in their innate, God-given talent and calling. Be prepared to be inspired in your personal, business, and spiritual life as you engage this book."
ELAINE YODER, DMin in leadership and spiritual formation, counselor at Life Counseling Ministries

"*The Serving Leader's Guide to Effective Meetings* is a very valuable tool in the toolbox of any leader who leads a group of people. If you lead an organization, business, committee, management team, or a family meeting, this book gives practical advice and articulates well the fundamentals of making your meetings more effective and efficient. Meetings themselves can be a demise to a project or organization's purpose. This reading gives a clear guide in logistics, agenda, resources, and the environment to fit the type of meeting you prepare. Merle takes a Biblical and Christlike approach in his perspective in this presentation about conducting your meetings. Merle's experience in business, business training, and leadership in Anabaptist Financial brings clarity in addressing this subject."
KEN BURKHOLDER, Business consultant

"Christian leaders are called to be servants, and this book shows Christian leaders how to serve their people by conducting meetings with proficiency and purpose. Drawing from his own story, Merle shows how to move meetings from chaos, inefficiency, and lack of engagement to order, purpose, and buy-in for everyone. Merle has been a friend for years, and I've known him as one who loves to learn. I'm delighted that he is willing to share what he has learned about conducting meetings. This is a very needed book for leaders who are serious about conducting proficient meetings as a service to their people."
JOHN COBLENTZ, Campus pastor of Faith Builders Educational Programs

"From his own story of failure and growth to wisdom gained from Amish businessmen, nonprofit leaders, and most importantly, the Bible, Merle has written an interesting, insightful, and practical book for anyone who leads or participates in meetings. The book goes beyond simply telling us what to do; instead, it calls us to examine who we are. I'll be turning to this book to sharpen my ability to serve well."
PATRICK HEATWOLE, School administrator at Miami Christian Academy

Foreword

Some time ago we needed to replace our kitchen sink. I asked a trusted acquaintance for help in deciding which sink to install. I thought the sink he recommended was outrageously expensive. Then, I remembered two things. First, Cynthia, my wife, would use this sink several times each day. Every day. For years. And second, I remembered that very recently I had spent a similar amount of money for a tool that would seldom be used. And the price hadn't seemed bad at all. Obviously, my value system needed some rearranging.

Meetings are like the kitchen sink—often out-of-mind and under-valued. Because meetings are so common, it is easy to assume we have more competence in leading meetings than we do. However, the people who attend meetings know the difference between a leader who treats meetings as a necessary evil and the leader who has honed the skill of effective meetings. Like the kitchen sink, effectively leading meetings is not a skill that slumbers in the toolbox. It makes sense, then, to invest a significant chunk of time and energy into acquiring that skill. The guide you are holding is the perfect tool for making a concentrated effort at developing as a meeting leader. If the skill wasn't so universally applicable, it may not deserve the kind of in-depth treatment Merle gives it. But leading effective meetings is like a nail gun to a carpenter or a trowel to a brick mason. Invest early and deeply in honing this vital skill. The dividends will pour in for the rest of your life.

Over the years I have been with Merle in many meetings, some formal and some unstructured. He led some of these meetings, participated in others. Either way, he generally brings a high level of preparation, energy, and engagement. At times during a discussion, he grows quiet. That generally means he is working on a line of thought that hasn't emerged yet. I especially appreciate the attention Merle gives to the personal, relational component of meetings. In all these ways, Merle practices what he preaches.

STEVEN BRUBAKER, *Administrator of Faith Builders Educational Programs*

Preface

For many years, I led inept and disorganized meetings. You will read about how I slowly faced the truth and began the journey to revolutionize my meetings. Serving as the CEO in a series of start-up organizations, I saw firsthand how a developing organization can quickly outgrow its current practice of meetings. Confused, I felt stymied and didn't know how to adopt better meeting practices.

Even after admitting and owning the looseness and ineffectiveness of my meetings, I seemingly couldn't break my deeply entrenched meeting habits. I floundered. Out of my shame of decades of mismanaged meetings, a passion was born to change and renovate them. It didn't take long to realize that I needed more than just passion; I needed knowledge of meeting principles and meeting skills. Even more than meeting principles and skills, my character needed to develop and change.

After committing to reform the way I led meetings, it took several years to redesign and restructure them—not to mention the character adjustments I needed throughout the process. By leading various companies, each became a laboratory to engineer, test-drive, fail, and reevaluate meetings.

Over time, the practical changes were drastic, but so were the end results. They leveraged my time and drastically reduced management overload. More importantly, relationships strengthened and a team spirit prevailed. A palpable trust emerged within teams because everyone felt free to bring problems to the table. Meetings became an anticipated activity, rich with connection. This didn't mean that healthy debate, constructive criticism, and emotional pain were absent. Instead, life-giving meetings welcomed people to be real and bring up their most troublesome issues at work.

While this guide promises to help structure, simplify, and systematize meetings, it also promises to help serving leaders run effective meetings by putting people first and staying connected to their hearts. It's a guide that values people relating to each other with trust, love, and graciousness, treating each man and woman around the table as a peer and equal. It will also help you achieve focused, synergistic meetings that extract the collective wisdom of a team—the embodied wisdom of Christ.

Your Guides

There is no replacement for life experience. As such, this guide draws from a wealth of real-life experiences from Anabaptist businesses such as Country Value Woodworks, Pioneer Equipment, and Seven Oaks Landscaping, as well as my own business, AgSalt Processing (see business biographies). These businesses exemplify the journey and search to lead stronger meetings and are a trove of common sense and skillful application of Christian values and relationships. My own experiences are embedded too and will carry you through the painful lessons I learned.

This guide also draws on the wisdom of some of the most respected experts currently in the field, such as Patrick Lencioni, Elise Keith, Michael Hyatt, Mark Horstman, and others. All these authors along with their peers have raised the bar for meetings and contributed to the growing body of literature available on the subject. I've attempted to incorporate the best of what I've learned from them into this content—combining their expert advice with my years of experience as a meeting practitioner.

Layout of the Content

To make it easier for you to grasp meeting concepts and practices, this guide is divided into five sections.

The first section unveils the serving leader difference and a Biblical perspective on meetings. If you're a Christian, likely you want your life to be consistent with Christian virtues. Without Holy Spirit-infused character, leaders shouldn't expect to achieve the high bar of meetings taught in this guide.

The subsequent three sections present the three-dimensional (3D) approach to meetings: the disciplines, the types, and the levels of meetings. It's a simple yet powerful meeting system that can be applied to any organization, large or small.

The "Meeting Disciplines" section provides guidance on the structure and skills needed to run great meetings. There are five disciplines taught in this guide: structure, facilitation, engagement, synergy, and ownership. These five disciplines are the heart and soul of this guide and will provide a high degree of insight into what skills are crucial to make meetings effective.

The "Meeting Types" section provides clarity to different kinds of meetings and how to create a meeting system to run an organization. There are three types of meetings: foundational, building-block, and relational. Knowing the difference between these three types and their interrelatedness enables a leader to construct a set of meetings to serve the needs of the organization.

The "Meeting Levels" section describes the horsepower and level of skill needed to support the size or complexity of an organization. There are three levels of meetings: basic, intermediate, and advanced. This guide demonstrates the difference between low-powered meetings that require basic meeting skills and knowledge and high-powered meetings.

Depending on the weight of the organizational load, more horsepower will need to be applied to meeting skills.

The final section of the guide, the "Step-by-Step Meeting Guides," will walk you through several key types of meetings, making the application of the meeting disciplines taught in this guide actionable. This section should feel like a coach by your side. It provides rich details and nuances of meeting practices and offers tips using a step-by-step approach.

Some readers prefer to read the introduction and then jump to the parts of the book that are most relevant to them. I understand—I do that too. To get the most out of this guide, however, I recommend that you start at the beginning and work straight through each chapter to the end.

An Anabaptist Christian Perspective

I'm an ordinary leader who learned in the trenches of trial and error. But I have an extraordinary interest in servant-led meetings. This guide is written from Anabaptist Christian roots, and you'll likely sense that the theological framework mirrors a deep identity with a people who have embraced suffering as one of the key catalysts of Christian transformation. We practice love and submission to God and brother as a chief trademark of character and the highest virtue of our faith—reaching far beyond the walls of worship—meaning our faith tradition is strong in practical, everyday living.

This guide will help serving leaders custom design and run meetings that not only embody Christian values but also increasingly exhibit efficiency and effectiveness. I care that you don't get the impression, however, that I promote serving leadership merely because it is effective. Some authors promote this way of leading simply because it works and because it's powerful. An Anabaptist and Christian understanding of serving leadership includes a not-so-popular posture toward one's followers—a sacrificial one. Approaching meetings as a true serving leader will cost you dearly. It will require you to admit your selfishness, embrace your weaknesses, and confess your sin. That's hard. That's suffering.

I want leaders to aspire to lead like Jesus and gain traction in their businesses. The following guide will not only inspire you to practice serving leadership based on bedrock Christian principles but also help you tap into a life-giving, Spirit-filled approach to meetings. Maybe that sounds like cliché religious jargon, but hear me out. The journey to transform my meetings wasn't easy, cool, or all fun. It included a thorough renovation of character. Out of such character will naturally flow practical meeting applications such as defined, structured, relationally rich discussions, and a systematic set of meetings that will transform your leadership.

After thousands of meetings, I'm eager to share my insights.

Table of Contents

The Serving Leader Difference

Chapter One
A Meeting Wake-Up Call

The ear that listens to life-giving reproof will dwell among the wise.
Whoever ignores instruction despises himself, but he who listens to
reproof gains intelligence.

PROVERBS 15:31-32

Back in the day when my company AgSalt Processing had only a couple of employees, we didn't have structured meetings. Meetings were shapeless and took the form of pop-up conversations—a question here, an extended discussion there, a decision made on the fly. In my head, information was gathered and sorted, with decisions made as I went along. It felt extremely efficient because I was always working, never wasting any time in meetings, keeping people engaged in "real work." When businesses are small with a few employees, running everything inside your head can be feasible if the leader is on-site and working side by side with everyone.

Such days were long gone for AgSalt. I was off-site most of the time and involved at a management level with multiple organizations. Without a thoughtfully designed structure for AgSalt's meetings, the leadership team felt a lack of cohesion and direction as a company. Critical information and plans were stored in the recesses of multiple people's heads. Some knew what was happening; others were clueless by no fault of their own. In the early days it had worked, but change was long overdue.

My two business partners, Doug and Dalen, were patient men, so they didn't complain—at first. Without warning one day, Dalen spoke out: "We're fed up with the disorganized and chaotic way you lead the company. You seem unaware of how this affects day-to-day operations." Dalen paused to add effect.

Caught off guard, I stuttered and asked, "What—what do you mean?" My mind raced to imagine what was coming next. I was the president of the company but absent from most day-to-day operations. I enjoyed the privilege of leading off-site because it allowed me to live in two worlds: my own for-profit company, AgSalt, and leadership positions within multiple nonprofit organizations. Our management arrangement was unique and had been agreed upon by everyone.

When Dalen paused, my other partner Doug jumped into the conversation, almost as if they had rehearsed the lines. But nothing was rehearsed—it was raw emotion salted with truth. "There's too much chaos and pressure. I'm tired of the strain! And we're stuck with a lack of clarity and direction. We're not pulling together in an organized way." I knew Doug liked things organized, though he rarely complained. With intensity in his voice, he finished, "We want something different."

At this point in the conversation my adrenaline was running strong, and I was sweating. I could tell their frustration had finally found an outlet, but there was more coming. Dalen resumed, "You're not bringing your best to the table. You're leading multiple organizations because you're a talented entrepreneur, but we're getting what's left of you— and it's not working. The other organizations like you because you're giving them your best, but we're seeing your worst!" By this time, I wasn't just sweating; I felt my one leg beginning to shake under the table. That wasn't a good sign because I was slipping into fear.

I knew two things. First, I sensed they weren't done venting and likely had dozens of examples to make their points stronger. Second, the charge that I was only giving a meager effort to AgSalt rang completely true. It was shocking, nonetheless, to hear them say so! My second leg started shaking.

What ensued was a two-hour, straight-shooting conversation. I was surprised when my fear subsided part way through the meeting and my legs quit shaking. I didn't feel falsely accused and even though they were saying hard things, it was a relief to admit to my part of the problem. The more questions I asked to understand how they felt, the deeper the trouble seemed to go. Toward the end of the confrontation, it became apparent no apology or even a heartfelt confession was going to fix the problem. It wasn't my past failure they were bothered about; it was the future. AgSalt was growing far too fast for an off-site president to be serving "leftovers" as the regular leadership meal.

Finally, at the end of the conversation, the real question was laid out by Dalen. "We need more of you—a lot more. What are you going to do to fix this problem?" Without my permission, my leg started shaking again.

I cleared my throat to speak, but I wouldn't have needed to. I didn't have an answer. After a moment of uncomfortable silence, Doug clinched the point by saying, "We don't believe you can turn this ship around with your current level of commitment to the business."

> " **Leaders who hate meetings are unconsciously projecting that they've fallen out of love with leadership.** "

I knew my partners were right. I was leading several fast-growing organizations and didn't have enough time, insight, or character to deliver the leadership strength AgSalt needed. It seemed only a silver bullet could save me. I left that meeting with two feelings. First, I felt grateful to Doug and Dalen for speaking the hard truth in love—a wake-up call. Second, I felt shaken with shame. Why had I overextended myself? Why was my leadership so inconsistent, with AgSalt getting the short end of the stick? With no positive answers, the ride home was hard. I was left with a sinking feeling of my inability. I grappled with the question, "What is the one thing that could make the most difference for AgSalt?"

From Death by Meeting to Life-Giving Meetings

Maybe you've grown cynical about meetings— and for good reason. In *Death by Meeting*, a book that has resonated with many people, author Patrick Lencioni explains how bad meetings themselves are not so much the problem; instead, it's a poor management philosophy. Leaders who hate meetings are unconsciously projecting that they've fallen out of love with leadership. They've forgotten why they chose leadership in the first place.

3

Meetings become unpleasant, taxing, frustrating, and—well, deathlike—when they aren't designed for the people and by the people. Meetings can feel like drudgery when participants are entrenched in bad habits. Maybe your meetings are average, mildly frustrating, but a long way from deathlike. Regardless, accurately identifying your current reality about meetings will help you step towards better meetings. After all, the ultimate expression of Christian leadership is to lead people as they seek or follow Christ, including in the workplace. Just like Christ gathered His disciples, so must leaders gather their people. It's a ripe place for transformation.

If meetings are consistently disappointing, even deathlike, it's because Christ's two life-giving priorities, loving God and loving your neighbor, are too weak or absent. Sin and weakness touch everything, and meetings are not immune. Lack of love and the associated vices of pride, fear, and alienation are anathema to meetings. These are root problems that lead to "death."

In meetings that lack the presence and power of Christ, attendees are disconnected and even alienated from one another. Instead of mutual support and camaraderie, people feel distant, shielded, and disengaged. As such, they don't share their best ideas but instead sit quietly, hiding their deepest thoughts. Instead of cooperation and synergy, participants strain in opposite directions and become mired in the mud of distrust and disagreement. Instead of finding momentum and unity for achieving common goals, vibrant visions for the future simply die.

Key purposes of a meeting are to:

- connect as a team to experience group synergy
- achieve understandings as a group
- solve problems
- make decisions
- hold each other accountable
- monitor progress towards goals
- debate in a healthy way that reaps the wisdom of "a multitude of counselors" (Proverbs 15:22 NKJV)

Effective, servant-led meetings are designed around purpose and structure. When facilitated skillfully they make room for healthy discussion and collaboration. It's no secret that life-giving marriages, families, and church congregations pulsate with love, trust, and humility; the same is true of meetings.

Three Fundamentals for Leading Great Meetings

There are three fundamentals you need for leading effectively: (1) the exponential effect, (2) powerful presence, and (3) Spirit-infused character.

The Exponential Effect

In *The Advantage: Why Organizational Health Trumps Everything Else in Business*, Patrick Lencioni states this:

> No action, activity, or process is more central to a healthy organization than the meeting. There's no better way to have a fundamental impact on an organization than by changing the way it does meetings.[1]

Why do meetings influence everything? The quality of your meetings is the root that yields a thousand consequences, good or bad. When you improve meetings, almost everything is affected. Improved meetings should produce better perspectives, better problem-solving, and better accountability—leading to better decisions. When we work together at the hub of the organization, it drives action that produces an exponential effect: a highly leveraging activity.

Powerful Presence

Leonard Meador, an experienced business consultant within the Anabaptist community, remembers being present in a meeting with a family in Nebraska. An older woman was left as sole heir of a large family farming operation, and she didn't feel equipped to run it. She called a family meeting which she opened with a humble appeal to her sons, sons-in-law, and daughters-in-law. "I'm not skilled in business," she said, "so I'll need your help." As she wrote on the whiteboard all the things she would need help with, Leonard recalled, "I was reduced to tears at the response. She was

creating a support team rather than fostering a competitive experience between the siblings. At the end of the meeting, we had an action list that was meaningful and a team of helpers who were motivated." Leonard's tears over his client's humble approach to leading her family point to the ingredients of a powerful meeting—God's presence and the unity of hearts tuned to each other.

Why are such meetings potentially powerful?

First, meetings are the place where two or more people discuss, debate, discern, and finally decide on a future course of action. Meetings, whether formal or informal, are where decisions are ultimately made, and the direction and course of the company are set.

Second, meetings are a sacred place where God desires to be present. When human and divine presence converge in meetings, powerful outcomes can be possible. God presides over meetings when He's invited to do so. If you want powerful meetings, start by gathering in His Name and seeking His presence. On the other hand, nothing disintegrates the power of presence more quickly than when a person is somewhere else in spirit. Undivided attention with one another, and with God's presence center stage, sets the environment for powerful meetings.

Spirit-Infused Character

The key to unlocking great meetings is to live out a set of Spirit-infused disciplines that transform negative human tendencies and release powerful human synergy with others. God's Spirit presiding over and around a meeting is one thing, but when His Spirit transforms the hearts and minds of the participants—that revolutionizes a meeting.

Great meetings don't happen by virtue of merely honing the skills taught in this guide. In fact, true serving leadership cannot be reached without character transformation through Christ. If leaders have not allowed the Spirit to infuse their character, even with a strong commitment to learn and practice meeting skills, they cannot tap into the heart of serving leadership. The disciplines taught in this guide count on transformed character to deliver the ultimate results. A meeting full of characters, lacking character, cannot be remedied. On the other hand, meetings conducted with Spirit-infused character and practiced meeting skills are some of the most productive and fulfilling activities in an organization.

These three fundamentals of meetings—the exponential effect, powerful presence, and Spirit-infused character—are the bedrock principles. The most sobering of them all is the idea that the quality of meetings is directly driven by the maturity and Holy Spirit-infused character of people at the table. No tool can help people in meetings who are bent on ignoring the principles of relationship and synergy. Not surprisingly, this meeting guide is based on the fundamental belief that the person and principles of Christ transform people—and hence their meetings.

The Call of the Serving Leader

What sets this meeting guide apart from others is a servant posture from a Christian perspective. Sometimes the problem in meetings isn't just a lack of structure, skill, and knowledge. The elephant in the room is often a lack of Christian character that no one will admit to. By contrast, when leaders possess the fullness of the Holy Spirit coupled with mature character, the difference in the meeting is palpable. I'm convinced one cannot aspire to servant leadership—and achieve it—unless a radical self-emptying and inner transformation occurs. This deliverance from one's self-serving bent comes only to those suffering with Christ. Out of suffering and sacrifice come a reshaping of character, receiving its identity and capacity *only* through life from God. Many come to Christ for the gift of heaven; fewer come to Christ for the gift of transformation, which always brings suffering. May those few sacrificial serving leaders become the leaders of the world. All other types of leadership should find another name.

> " Out of suffering and sacrifice come a reshaping of character, receiving its identity and capacity *only* through life from God. "

Jesus connected to the hearts of His disciples by teaching them and showing them a servant is not greater than his master. And yet, as their master, He fell to His knees and washed their feet. May Jesus's example encourage you to do the same in your company.

Chapter Two

A Biblical Perspective on Meetings

*One thing have I asked of the LORD, that will I seek after: that I
may dwell in the house of the LORD all the days of my life, to gaze
upon the beauty of the LORD and to inquire in his temple.*

PSALM 27:4

Imagine what it must have been like for the Israelites in the wilderness
witnessing God's presence in the Tabernacle of Meeting. As God
visibly came to meet Moses in the pillar of cloud, it rested in front of the
door of the tent as He met with their leader.

"Thus the LORD used to speak to Moses face to face, as a man speaks
to his friend" (Exodus 33:11). Moses had become overwhelmed with
the burden of leading the people, and he was concerned that he could
not "bring up this people" (33:12) without more concrete evidence that
God would do His part! At the
Tabernacle of Meeting, Moses
pleaded, "If I have found favor
in your sight, please show me
now your ways, that I may
know you in order to find favor
in your sight" (33:13). Moses
goes even one step further to
complain that "this nation is
your people" (33:13). This was
a bold lament pushing the
problem upon God to take
responsibility and ownership
of these difficult people. Then
God's reply satisfied Moses:
"My presence will go with
you, and I will give you rest"

> " The indwelling Spirit of
> God is the differentiator
> in life-giving meetings,
> and one of its most
> tangible expressions is
> participants fully engaged
> and deeply synergized
> with each other. "

(33:14). Moses replied with one last assertion to drive his point home, "If
your presence will not go with me, *do not* bring us up from here" (33:15,
emphasis added). Moses somehow knew that if he did not get the
promise of God's presence, his efforts and leadership would never make
the grade. For Moses, God's favor, guidance, and grace were wrapped up
in one reality—God's presence.

In the account above, it almost seems as if Moses had to twist God's arm
to promise His presence. In the New Testament, however, the presence

of God is readily available when His people gather. Jesus said, "For where two or three are gathered in my name, there am I among them" (Matthew 18:20). The context for this promise of presence is working out offenses and issues in a brotherly fashion. God's presence makes the profound difference even in a tough meeting if the group truly meets in His Name, bearing the torch of His presence in their hearts.

Instead of a pillar of cloud by day and fire by night to display God's presence and guidance, today we have His presence in our hearts. "Do you not know that your body is a temple of the Holy Spirit within you, whom you have from God?" (1 Corinthians 6:19). The indwelling Spirit of God is the differentiator in life-giving meetings, and one of its most tangible expressions is participants fully engaged and deeply synergized with each other.

The presence of the Lord can seem intangible and ineffective in a meeting. But remember, God's glory and presence radically transformed and affected the meeting with Moses, overshadowing the door to the Tabernacle of Meeting with a cloud. And after Moses got persistent, God promised that His presence would go with Moses as he led the people! God may no longer show up in meetings the way He dramatically did in the Old Testament, embodied in a pillar of cloud or fire. He is now present in a new way—living inside of us. Three cornerstone practices make up the new and greater way of God's presence transforming meetings: dwelling, gazing, and washing.

The Dwelling Cornerstone

How does the cornerstone of dwelling relate to a Biblical perspective on meetings? What does it mean to dwell? The concept of dwelling is used widely in Scripture and often means residing in the house or area where one lives. In a relational sense, it also means to live together in close proximity. One of God's promises to David was, "I will dwell among the children of Israel and will not forsake my people Israel" (1 Kings 6:13). At the dedication of the temple, Solomon exclaimed, "I have built you an exalted house, a place for you to dwell in forever" (2 Chronicles 6:2). However, in the New Testament we learn that "the Most High does not dwell in houses made by hands" (Acts 7:48). And finally, Paul makes the climactic declaration: "that Christ may dwell in your hearts through faith" (Ephesians 3:17).

I'm using the concept of dwelling as a metaphor to denote being rooted in relationship, securing a steadfast connection, and taking responsibility. God's Spirit is rooted and fused in a union with our spirit; indeed, He dwells. In a relational sense, to dwell with each other means to put down roots by being fully committed and yielded to stay with others over a long period of time. To dwell means to become bonded, attached, and belong to others with a healthy sense of emotional security. This looks like stepping into a meeting with a heartfelt sense that "I belong here" and "I belong to you." To dwell means to drive down the stakes of identity, saying, "I'm all in" and taking your place at the table where you take responsibility for the meeting.

By contrast, when only warm bodies show up in a meeting, present in body but absent in spirit, it is the antithesis to the meaning of *dwelling*. In this negative sense, people attend meetings as spectators and not as players. Neither yielded to others nor united, they let the responsibility of success fall to someone else in the meeting. They attend, but remain aloof, separate, and emotionally alienated from the group to some degree. They sit in meetings like squatters did in the western frontier days of America during the 1800s. They would occupy a place but wouldn't invest in true ownership of and responsibility for it. This couldn't be further from David's expectation for people to dwell: "Behold, how good and pleasant it is when brothers dwell in unity!" (Psalm 133:1) Instead of squatting, the practice of dwelling in meetings requires participants to fully own the meeting and make the down payment of emotionally driving down stakes of high-trust relationships with those at the same table.

> " When members truly dwell with each other, people are linked up, synced up, and spiritually attuned— not merely mentally focused. "

First Corinthians 12 and 13 are likely the most instructive chapters in Scripture on dwelling in unity and should inform and guide meetings. "For just as the body is one and has many members, and all the members of the body, though many, are one body, so it is with Christ… Now you are the body of Christ and individually members of it" (1 Corinthians 12:12, 27). The human body is a metaphor for the body of Christ as well as mirroring the meeting with many individual members operating in sync. This group has a diverse range of gifts, talents, and abilities—each offering the same care and love for one another.

When gathering, we often raise the question of "How are you?" as a surface way to connect. But the question of dwelling and presence is much deeper. God's first question in the garden of Eden was, "Where are you?" (Genesis 3:9). Adam and Eve had pulled up their stakes and hidden, alienating themselves from God because of their shame. "Where are you?" is a profound identity question inquiring about the foundations of your loyalty and bonds, those which Adam and Eve had just violated. Instead of "How are you?" the deeper questions are "Where are you?" and "Are you dwelling?" To dwell, then, means to come into a meeting with others, not hiding even if you have just failed. It means closing the door to the whirlwind of distractions and entering the meeting armed against the enemy of interruptions. When members truly dwell with each other, people are linked up, synced up, and spiritually attuned—not merely mentally focused. Paul said, "You also are being built together into a dwelling place for God by the Spirit" (Ephesians 2:22). As such, when meetings are built as a dwelling place, the participants become an expression of the living, breathing body of Christ—literally, the presence of Christ.

GAZE

The Gazing Cornerstone

When Moses experienced the overwhelming presence of God by the overshadowing cloud of His presence, he wanted more. He pleaded for one final thing. "Please show me your glory" (Exodus 33:18). Note that Moses did not directly ask to see God's face. Ironically, the full blazing glory of God was only to be found there. And God answered accordingly, "You cannot [gaze upon] my face, for man shall not see me and live" (Exodus 33:20). But to honor Moses's longing to see His glory—the ultimate presence of God—He put Moses in the cleft of a rock and covered the cleft with His hand as He passed by. When He removed His hand, Moses stepped out and saw the back of God. Exodus 34 ends with Moses descending from Mount Sinai with his face shining.

The apostle Paul recounts the shining of Moses's face as "the glory of his countenance" (2 Corinthians 3:7 NKJV). God's presence in the Old Testament was expressed in multiple ways, such as the pillar of cloud by day and fire by night. But it was equally expressed in Moses by his glowing facial countenance. Moses veiled his face "so that the children of Israel could not look steadily at the end of what was passing away" (3:13). But the people's "minds were blinded" (3:14). Paul uses this physical expression of God's glory through the face of Moses to point to the future ministry of the Spirit in us.

> " To gaze with the liberty of the Spirit on the countenance of real unveiled human faces is to see a glimpse of divine presence. "

With the indwelling Spirit, the "veil of Moses" is taken away. This means there is liberty and complete freedom to look steadily and gaze at the glory of the Lord as revealed in unveiled faces of people born of the Spirit! "Where the Spirit of the Lord is, there is liberty" (2 Corinthians 3:17 NKJV). This is an important spiritual and relational breakthrough—privileged access to the glory of the Lord by beholding the unveiled face.

What does Paul mean, "beholding as in a mirror the glory of the Lord" (2 Corinthians 3:18 NKJV)? To gaze with the liberty of the Spirit on the countenance of real unveiled human faces is to see a glimpse of divine presence. To behold the glory of the Lord in another is to drink in their presence and be moved emotionally and receive spiritual encouragement. Paul says, "And we all, with unveiled face" (3:18). This term *unveiled face* is not only a metaphor of an inner spiritual unveiled heart or renewed mind. It can certainly include that, but unveiled face also denotes physical faces with real skin. Moses's face was real skin but miraculously reflected the shining glory of the Lord to the people. In a comparable manner, yet "more glorious" (3:11), people who are indwelt by the Spirit should physically reflect their unveiled heart and transformed mind on their countenance! What you do with your face matters.

My four-year-old daughter made this point in a dramatic fashion. I had her on my lap, and she wanted my absolute attention and presence. I was mostly distracted, shifting my eyes and not holding eye contact except for a second or two. She was talking to me, but my face was veiled. Finally, she grabbed my chin and turned my face to directly align with hers. "Look at me!" she pleaded. She continued to hold my chin, squeezing tightly so I couldn't turn my face away from hers. As she held my face, forcing me to hold eye contact, I soon became uncomfortable as she poured out her story that she wanted me to hear. She wanted a lot more than for me to just passively listen and mentally focus on her story.

My four-year-old taught me a deep lesson. I had a habit of shutting off the full force of my presence, attention, and inner spirit by looking away and breaking eye contact. She did not realize how grabbing my chin and holding my face to gaze at her was a powerful, innocent rebuke of a lifelong habit. I believe she wanted to feel the presence of the Lord—the glory of my countenance. She wanted me to intently listen and be moved in my soul with her story.

In addition to eye contact, unveiled faces are expressive faces, not deadpan or flat. To gaze

> " As we reflect the presence of the Lord in each other's faces and engage through our countenance in everyday, ordinary organizational meetings, we are mysteriously transformed and our presence becomes weightier. "

doesn't mean to gawk, stare, or glare, but rather to look steadfastly so as to connect emotionally and spiritually with the presence of another. Unveiled faces are alive and radiant, sending and receiving clear relational signals to those around them. As such, love, compassion, and delight stream out of the eyes of our countenance and into the heart. The countenance of the face is a powerful behavior but only if it is used! Nothing kills a meeting more quickly than when no one is gazing into the eyes—into the soul and spirit. When we quench the Spirit with listless stares and lifeless eyes, the die of the meeting is cast. As Moses longed to see more of the presence of God, we too should yearn to see the glory of Jesus on the unveiled faces of others.

The unveiled faces of Spirit-filled people should play a part in transforming relationships. When faces light up with expressive facial messages coming from deep within the soul, people feel loved, seen, known, and valued simply for their presence. The power of an accepting look or the sparkle of the eye expressing delight can richly feed the soul—and strengthen relationship. Holding a respectful concentrated gaze with the person speaking is a practical application of keeping your face unveiled. Conversely, veiled faces are constantly distracted, looking around the room, and breaking eye contact, diverting their eyes from the person speaking. As we reflect the presence of the Lord in each other's faces and engage through our countenance in everyday, ordinary organizational meetings, we are mysteriously transformed and our presence becomes weightier—"from one degree of glory to another" (2 Corinthians 3:18).

The Washing Cornerstone

Consider also the most famous meeting of all, the Last Supper, when Jesus gave His disciples His Upper Room Discourse. How Jesus conducted that meeting offers important lessons for serving leaders:

> *Jesus, knowing that the Father had given all things into his hands, and that he had come from God and was going back to God, rose from supper. He laid aside his outer garments, and taking a towel, tied it around his waist. Then he poured water into a basin and* began to wash the disciples' feet *and to wipe them with the towel that was wrapped around him. (John 13:3–5, emphasis added)*

And when Jesus concludes this feet washing moment, He tells us why He did it:

> *When he had washed their feet and put on his outer garments and resumed his place, he said to them,* "Do you understand what I have done to you? *You call me Teacher and Lord, and you are right, for so I am. If I then, your Lord and Teacher, have washed your feet, you also ought to wash one another's feet.* For I have given you an example, that you also should do just as I have done to you. *Truly, truly, I say to you, a servant is not greater than his master, nor is a messenger greater than the one who sent him. If you know these things,* blessed are you if you do them." *(John 13:12–17, emphasis added)*

The practices of dwelling and gazing are two cornerstones on which to begin building a meeting culture. To this foundation, Jesus adds the third cornerstone of washing each other's feet. Anyone serious about leading like Jesus must reckon with this central teaching. My religious tradition of Anabaptism employs the physical practice of feet washing as part of the communion worship service. As with any rich worship ceremony, its spiritual power ripples out to encompass all of life. Washing each other's feet has application in many aspects of life, including meetings.

In the broadest sense, kneeling to wash another's feet represents serving others' needs by lifting up, empowering, and counting others more significant than yourself (Philippians 2:3). Jesus provides a more specific meaning when Peter resisted Him washing his feet. When Jesus stipulated, "If I do not wash you, you have no share with me" (John 13:8), Peter reacted and missed the whole point with a request to wash not only his feet but also his hands and head. "Jesus said to him, 'The one who has bathed does not need to wash, except for his feet, but is completely clean. And you are clean, but not every one of you.' For he knew who was to betray him; that was why he said, 'Not all of you are clean'" (John 13:10–11).

Feet washing was a practical cleaning of dirty feet after walking on dusty paths. Jesus used the very familiar custom of His day to point to the common spiritual dirt of the soul. As such, one practical application of feet washing involves helping to wash off each other's spiritual, emotional, and behavioral dirt (see illustration 1). Washing someone's feet can include getting down to the regret and shame of each other's lives. Feet washing is helping each other to clean the inside (heart, mind, attitude, motives) and the outside (behaviors, words, acts, deeds). This could look like listening to regrets, mistakes, and frustrations of the team and offering encouragement. It could go deeper to include hearing confessions, understanding lifelong patterns, bearing another's grief, and offering empathy and compassion. The reverse is equally true. Allowing someone else to wash your feet can look like seeking out another to listen and help with your weaknesses, inabilities, and fears. It can go deeper, inviting team members to help you identify and admit sin, lifelong habits, and failures that affect your leadership and meetings. If you've been around leaders for very long, one glaring problem is shared: they're tempted to hide.

> " When leaders lay down their egos, take off their shoes, and ask for followers to wash their feet, it upends the leadership pyramid. "

Jesus's bold words to Peter echo to us today, "If I do not wash you, you have no share with me" (John 13:8). If we refuse like Peter to take off our shoes, to bring our sin, faults, and shame to be washed by our fellow believer, we have no part with Jesus. Who would eagerly sign up to invite

Illustration 1: A serving leader washes the feet of those they serve and humbly allows their own feet to be washed.

a brother or sister to literally get their hands dirty? Hiding makes perfect sense!

When leaders lay down their egos, take off their shoes, and ask for followers to wash their feet, it upends the leadership pyramid. As such, when leaders quit hiding their faults, it will likely shock their followers. Not that their followers didn't already know their faults, but they are stunned that a leader would humbly admit it and have the courage to ask for help to be cleansed and healed. Such heartfelt confession and humility is a far cry from the professional apology so glibly offered by leaders who admit fault with no real repentance, but only with the regret of a bruised ego.

How does this relate to meetings? We all bring our dirt to meetings: super-ficial connections, distracted presence, overbearing influence, unhealthy conflict, and undisciplined conversations. This list could go on. In these matters, leaders must go first and dare to get below the surface of running a meeting. Those who humbly ask for their soul to be washed, leading the way for character transformation, will find Jesus's promise true: "If you know these things, blessed are you if you do them" (John 13:17).

Common Grace

Many leaders run meetings that tap into principles of truth and good relationship without the three cornerstones above. They don't get fully present or engaged or yield to the power of synchronizing with others. They don't regularly reveal their faults, mistakes, and weaknesses. Not surprisingly, the glory of the Lord does not descend on such a meeting. Some meetings may still access common grace, however, and produce an effective meeting

> " Some Christian leaders use common grace—and mistake it as all there is— thus never tapping into the full measure of the Spirit available to them. "

outcome. Receiving common grace is not dependent on saving grace and a personal relationship with Jesus. This grace is experi-enced in people's lives when they unknowingly align with the principles of God or Scripture. Sometimes the Spirit works in the world enabling progress and good without possessing the hearts of mankind. In this sense, God's grace is poured out on all mankind whether Christian or non-Christian. In this way, common grace can show up in a meeting as wise planning, intelligent decision-making, and effective problem-solving—resulting in organi-zational and financial success. For example, when leaders cast a compelling, shared vision and draw others into the meaningful purpose of the mission, such meetings will likely motivate the group to achieve it. These meetings can be stripped of spiritual vitality, however, and as such are only a shell of what meetings could be if the Spirit was fully expressed through the participants' character, mindset, and emotions.

For the Christian, there should be no such thing as a meeting tapping only common grace, even if the subject matter doesn't directly reference spiritual things. Some Christian leaders use common grace—and mistake it as all there is—thus never tapping into the full measure of the Spirit available to them. Even so, leaders who run their meetings solely on common grace can keep their meetings out of dysfunction, but they are still subpar. These leaders stifle the fullness of the Spirit and never grow to their full stature of Christ, in their character, mindset, and emotional wisdom. By contrast, when the rich embodied grace of the Spirit flows out of participants and onto the meeting table, it should be noticeably different from what takes place in a meeting operating only on common grace.

Building the Foundation

Three cornerstones build a foundation for the serving leader to lead meetings. First, to experience the presence of the Lord in a meeting requires dwelling in unity with secure bonds of love, valuing each member's unique contribution. People offer their full measure in meetings if they are rooted, bonded, and secure in relationship with those around the table.

Second, a Biblical perspective on meetings requires offering the glory of our facial countenance and giving the gift of gazing upon others. With an unveiled face, a leader vibrantly reflects the indwelling Spirit with their full attention, engagement, understanding, passions, yearnings, feelings, and love. This transforms a meeting into a time of rich relational connections and group synergy.

> " Holy Spirit-infused character is often elusive, beyond the reach of many a leader's grasp! "

Finally, a Biblical approach to meetings necessitates that we bring our whole selves and quit hiding the warts and blemishes of our lives. This includes confessing our sins, failures, weaknesses, and mistakes. It means bringing the embarrassing shame of our lives into the sunlight for others to help wash and cleanse.

When meetings embody a culture in which these three cornerstones are present, such meetings reveal heavenly gems. Those around such a table become free, passionate, and highly motivated because hidden shame is gone. The power of God transforms people! Leading meetings takes mature character radiating the fruits of the Spirit. Holy Spirit-infused character is often elusive, beyond the reach of many a leader's grasp! The Holy Spirit will not control you like a robot. Rather, little by little, over decades of living out your faith, God's grace, power, and strength permeate your human capacities and become indistinguishable from you—infused into the warp and woof of your character!

Life-giving meetings ride on the character of the meeting leader. Give yourself time to apply and hone these foundational cornerstones. It is unrealistic to assume that mere knowledge of meeting principles and practices will translate into instant change. Meeting change is not microwaveable. Transforming meetings to reflect Biblical foundations requires discipline and practice. This journey may be hard, but it leads to lofty heights. I challenge you to be among those who dare to scale those heights.

Most people dislike meetings and for many good reasons, even to the point they secretly wish they could manage to run the company with fewer meetings. To this the Scriptures offer a counterpoint. We should not be "neglecting to meet together, as is the habit of some, but encouraging one another" (Hebrews 10:25). While this Scripture directly refers to meeting together as a local congregation, it seems appropriate to receive the same admonishment not to neglect meeting together in the workplace.

Meetings, especially organizational ones, are a place where God promises His presence. If people meet in His name, dwell together in unity, gaze at His glory with unveiled faces, and bring their basins and towels, the glory of the Lord shows up.

Meeting Disciplines

After twenty years, I still wasn't holding regular meetings at AgSalt. In those early years, we only had a few employees, and the random meeting was all I thought we needed. I'd long since left the family farm of my boyhood, but I was still running the business as if it were just the brothers and my dad. I didn't think meetings mattered. But things became complicated as AgSalt began to grow.

As more employees joined the company, the chaos, misunderstandings, and inefficiency only intensified. We hadn't yet identified our lack of meeting structure and design. In the beginning, our meetings were thrown together haphazardly, using the process of trial and error. As the years passed, I started other organizations where my meeting problems were reproduced. Keep in mind, it didn't seem meetings were a significant problem. If Doug and Dalen hadn't sounded a loud wake-up call, the haunting question would have never surfaced, "What is the one thing that could make the most difference for AgSalt?" If we hadn't hired a coach, we likely would have never discovered the answer to that question—which was meetings!

I was introduced to Ray Randolph, a consultant specializing in the Lean business culture, by my Amish friend Elam Esh from Country Value Woodworks. Elam explained how Ray had coached them over a period of five years and transformed their entire furniture manufacturing company into a Lean culture. For Elam, the odd surprise was Ray's insistence and help in rebuilding their inefficient meetings into an organized approach that served his people. Elam was so excited and inspired by Ray's work that he invited me to visit Country Value to see for myself the impact of servant-led meetings.

At that point, I'd led and participated in over a thousand meetings across multiple organizations. It seemed like I had seen it all. I didn't realize my blindness to obvious meeting problems and my lack of knowledge. I was about to witness firsthand what was happening at Country Value and how different Elam's meetings were from AgSalt's.

"My meetings didn't always look like this," Elam assured me. "This is what can happen when someone objective and disciplined like Ray pushes, critiques, and challenges you. You've got to love it when you're the problem."

Puzzled, I asked, "What do you mean?"

Elam continued, "If meetings need to change, guess who's responsible? The leader! And that was me!" Elam's comment sobered me and sparked the shame I still felt from my partners' searing critique of my leadership at AgSalt.

Once onboard as a coach with AgSalt, I assumed Ray would find the key problem to be our lack of Lean application in production. We were a manufacturing company packaging salt for the feed and ice melt industry. Ray did not disappoint as he applied his Lean expertise to our production processes. After sitting in one management meeting with the AgSalt leadership, however, he kindly but firmly suggested a complete meeting overhaul.

Elam's words echoed in my head, "You've got to love it when you're the problem." He had learned to look problems squarely in the face—and not lose heart, which encouraged me as I remembered his words. Ray began to challenge me to grow in the way I served and loved others by completely redesigning my meetings to be disciplined, structured, and people-centric. He revealed the keynote problem causing AgSalt's stress and chaos—meetings I led.

It was a painful process that completely disrupted my old haphazard way of leading meetings. Ray facilitated AgSalt's meetings for about a year, and I came to understand the value of enlisting help to learn how to properly conduct meetings. It was during this year that my leadership turned around. Left to myself, I would never have become aware that my meetings were causing the trouble. I may have been an old dog, but Ray was teaching me new tricks. One of those tricks was that my meetings needed to be guided by certain disciplines!

While leading great meetings is indeed challenging, it isn't mysterious or beyond the reach of the average leader. Great meetings boil down to the following five meeting disciplines, or competencies:

 **Meeting Structure**

 **Meeting Facilitation**

 **Meeting Engagement**

 **Meeting Synergy**

 **Meeting Ownership**

Chapter Three
Meeting Structure

The single biggest structural problem facing leaders of meetings is the tendency to throw every type of issue that needs to be discussed into the same meeting, like a bad stew with too many random ingredients.

PATRICK LENCIONI, *Death by Meeting*

Meetings need to be engineered and designed. Like machinery, design is everything. I grew up on a dairy farm in Pennsylvania in the late 60s and 70s. The design of machinery dramatically changed during the previous fifty years. Horse-drawn sickle mowers eventually gave way to tractor-drawn sickle-bar, which then advanced to the combined sickle-bar mower and conditioner. By the time I grew old enough to mow hay, innovative changes made the sickle-bar almost obsolete in the wake of the rotary disc mowers.

Like most equipment, meeting structure is improved with intentional research, innovation, and thoughtful design. Good meeting structure supports the meeting's purpose, writes the agenda, and addresses the action points. Structure can be defined as a threefold framework of preparing, leading, and following up after the meeting. These three phases are generic to most organizational meetings, and they guide which actions or steps are necessary.

> **" Structure is like an engine block; it turns firepower into horsepower. "**

A meeting, like anything involving the exercise of power, needs structure to express its full potential. Contemplate how the strength of an ox cannot be fully harnessed without a yoke, or how the bullet cannot hit its mark without the structure of the rifle barrel, and how human muscle cannot engage in movement without the rigid structure of a skeletal frame. Structure—as boring as it might sound—is like an engine block; it turns firepower into horsepower. Skillfully conducting meetings transfers horsepower into traction on the ground.

Let's be clear. Structure isn't meant to be so rigid it can't bend. It's important for servant-led meetings to remain people-oriented first and foremost. Meetings must glide on the rails of rich relationships and be considerate of others' input and ideas. There comes a time in meetings when breaking from the predetermined structure is a good idea. But in order to know when to bend the rules, you must first understand how they're applied.

The structure of any type of meeting has three basic phases:

1. preparing for the meeting
2. leading the meeting
3. following up after the meeting (see illustration 2)

Anything well-designed has been given appropriate consideration, with adequate forethought and research. Hence it requires "thinking about your meetings as though you were a designer," as Kevin Hoffman says in *Meeting Design: For Managers, Makers, and Everyone.*[2]

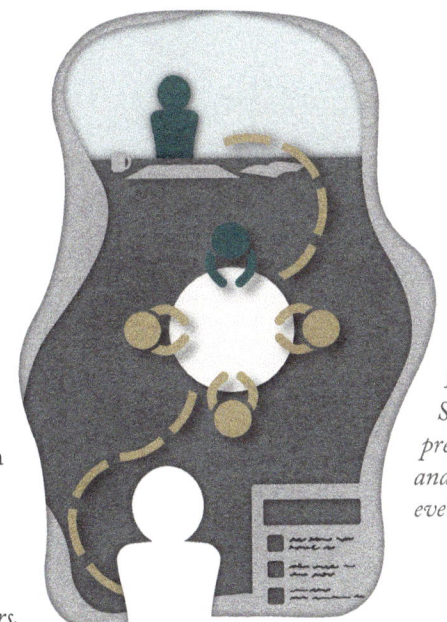

Illustration 2: Serving leaders prepare for, lead, and follow up after every meeting.

Preparing for the Meeting

Good preparation is often the best predictor of a great outcome. We've all been in meetings where participants were unprepared. Whether you're leading the meeting or just participating, honor those around you by being prepared. Know your role, familiarize yourself with the agenda, and review meeting documents in advance so you can bring value to the discussion. As educator Steven Brubaker has said, "To be worthwhile, most meetings need as much time in preparation and in follow-up as the meeting itself."[3]

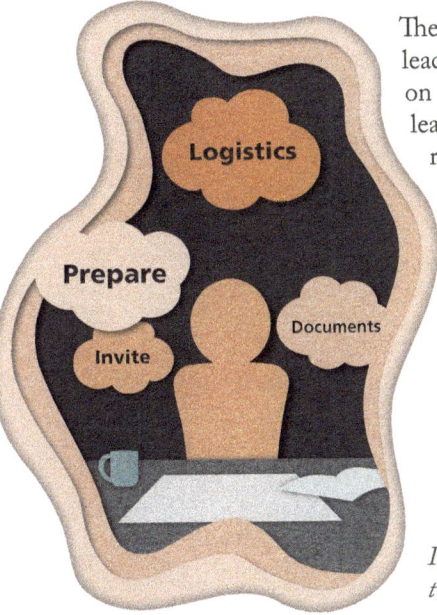

The following steps are a menu for leaders to choose from, depending on the type of meeting they're leading. Typically, good preparation requires five steps:

1. Plan the logistics.
2. Design the agenda.
3. Prepare the documents and resources.
4. Send the meeting invitation and agenda.
5. Prepare the participants and meeting space (see illustration 3).

Illustration 3: A serving leader sets aside time to adequately prepare for every meeting.

Step One: Plan the Logistics

Handling logistics requires answering the following questions:

Is the meeting needed? The first step in planning a meeting is determining whether the issues at hand could be handled another way. For example, could this meeting be replaced by an email exchange? What if only a subset of the group that typically meets gets an invitation? Would a short phone call with a few key people suffice? In *No-Fail Meetings*, Michael Hyatt writes:

> *As a rule, we're too quick to meet. When a question or problem pops up, it's easier to say, "Let's set up a meeting," than it is to spend a few brain cycles in the moment to solve the problem. In the process, we turn what might have been a ten-minute chat today into an hour-long meeting tomorrow.[4]*

In short, decide on what constitutes an effective, productive meeting for your team, and cancel all the rest.

What's the purpose of the meeting? What type of meeting is needed? These two questions are closely tied together because the reason you're calling the meeting informs the structure of the meeting. If you lead meetings regularly, you intuitively know meetings fall into two broad categories—regular and one-offs. The purpose of regular meetings is often preset and agreed upon in advance. If the purpose of a regular meeting is unknown or ambiguous, it's time to get clear or cross it off your calendar. A one-off meeting is scheduled for a specific and clear reason.

How far in advance should the meeting be scheduled? What day and time? Advanced scheduling enables leaders to plan their calendars weeks or months into the future and helps reserve important meeting dates. Different types of meetings require varied amounts of planning, so scheduling in advance is an important factor of logistics. On the agenda, always include the date and time of day the meeting will be held.

Who should be invited? Participation is often based on the role a person plays in the organization. For example, a weekly management meeting typically includes only people at the management level. However, at times a mix of participants will be brought together for special projects. For example, a product launch could bring together a diverse cross section of people. Or, in the event of a mediation meeting, a senior member of the company might be invited to weigh in, as their wisdom could aid in the resolution. Overall, the selection of participants for any meeting should be based on their

> **" Decide on what constitutes an effective, productive meeting for your team, and cancel all the rest. "**

position and responsibilities in the company, as well as their potential to effectively contribute to the desired outcome. Avoid participation for the sake of mere inclusion.

Who will lead the meeting? Who will take notes? Decide on a chairperson who will run the meeting and lead the team through the agenda. Designate a secretary to take notes, record important decisions, list and assign necessary tasks, and keep track of time. Separating the responsibilities for managing a meeting into two distinct roles will prevent overloading the chairperson and free him or her to lead the meeting. Certain smaller meetings, like those with only two or three participants, may not require secretarial tasks. The same is true for large meetings meant for company-wide announcements.

Where will the meeting be located? In the era of digital communication, people aren't always meeting physically. Be sure to include all details on how to attend virtual meetings. Also, some types of meetings are best held at another location for optimum focus and connection.

meeting logistics can be assumed and don't need to be listed, these items listed below must be clear in everyone's mind:

- name or title for the meeting
- date
- time
- location (including technical information, if virtual)
- attendees
- purpose of the meeting
- desired outcome
- chairperson for the meeting
- secretary for the meeting

This is a standard format for planning and announcing meetings. Including the name and a brief description of the purpose at the top of the meeting agenda is a simple practice that helps prepare participants to arrive at the meeting informed and with a clear understanding of why they need to participate. Remember, clarity conveys respect for the participants and people will feel supported and better able to prepare when meeting logistics are obvious.

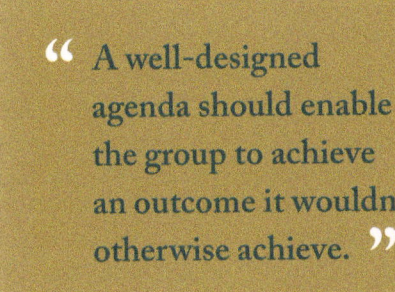

> " **A well-designed agenda should enable the group to achieve an outcome it wouldn't otherwise achieve.** "

2 Step Two: Design the Agenda

The agenda is a meeting's roadmap. Merely listing generic categories such as "opening remarks," "reports," "discussion points," and "tasks" is not the same as designing an agenda. Such terms may be appropriate as a framework to build upon, but always ask yourself if the agenda truly fits the type of meeting needed, and whether it will produce the desired outcomes.

When creating an agenda, consider the following questions:

What logistical information should appear on the agenda? Logistical information should appear at the top of the meeting's agenda. While some

Is the meeting's agenda designed to fit the type of meeting? The agenda must be tailored to fit the reason you are meeting. Consider carefully if a topic belongs on the agenda; some subjects are better addressed in other meetings. As a serving leader, guard your precious meeting time against distracting issues by asking, "Would any of these items be handled better within a different meeting?" A well-designed agenda should enable the group to achieve an outcome it wouldn't otherwise achieve. Regularly scheduled meetings often become stagnant when agenda items become rote and boring. This tends to happen when meetings are just part of the schedule, and planning falls victim to routine. Foster a lively meeting culture by changing things every now and then—keeping the process exciting, interesting, and enjoyable.

Are all agenda items clear, relevant, and sequential? First, identify the main points or categories and place them in an outline. Ensure these are clear and relevant to the type of meeting. Second, list subtopics under each main point or category. For example, often in management meetings the outline includes "discussion points" or "issues." Third, prioritize the list of agenda topics so they follow a logical sequence. This is a key principle in designing an agenda. A random arrangement of items will never produce the best results. Choose a sequence and flow for the items on the agenda in a way that the latter items naturally build upon the former, increasing the probability of momentum during discussion. This could mean the most important items don't necessarily go first, but they certainly should not go last.

Does each agenda item have a person assigned to present it? Is there a time limit on the agenda item? To come fully prepared, those presenting items on the agenda need to know in advance which items are theirs to lead. Indicate any time restraints next to the item if time is allocated, along with the presenter's name.

What unique facilitation approach or presentation method should be used? Design the agenda by choosing a facilitation approach that engages and brings the topic to life. For more detail on facilitating meetings, see chapter 4. Don't rely on simple dialogue as your only go-to facilitation approach. Instead, serve your people by using varied facilitation approaches that match the issue at hand. For example, drawing a concept on a whiteboard can aid in understanding. Facilitation approaches can be thought of as "knobs that you can twist to adjust to the culture of an individual meeting," as Kevin Hoffman puts it in *Meeting Design*.[5]

Do any participants have an item for the agenda? While the leader of the meeting is responsible to create the agenda and map out the meeting topics and items, participants may have input as well. Reach out to other attendees and ask if there is anything they would like to add or set a standard time for item submission.

3 Step Three: Prepare the Documents and Resources

Most meetings have information, reports, or data of some kind that will need to be prepared and brought to the meeting. Devise a process that makes the gathering of information seamless for each type of meeting in your organization. At Anabaptist Financial, a nonprofit I help lead, we use OneNote to digitally prepare and publish the agenda and to track our notes for each meeting. At AgSalt, we use Excel.

Consider the chairperson and secretary as a two-person team creating an efficient process by clarifying who does what in preparation. If printed agendas are used, typically the secretary is responsible for getting a copy to every team member and for bringing all other prepared documents to the meeting.

The following questions should be answered while preparing meeting documents:

Does an agenda item need visual aids? Visuals are some of the most powerful tools in a meeting, enabling all participants to simultaneously hear and see information. When reporting on numbers, reports are most always visual. Keep in mind that other items on the agenda could be greatly enhanced if visual information is used, not just when numbers are involved.

Does a presenter need to be coached or aided in preparing documents? If so, help them think about a clear and understandable way to present their information. For example, a mentor of mine redesigned a presentation involving complex calculations that had overwhelmed my peers upon initial delivery. After the document was cleaned up, the information was easily understood.

Do the documents need to be organized? Great meetings can happen with little or no documentation. I remember the early days of Anabaptist Financial's quarterly board meetings. A few stapled papers worked well. But over a decade later, board notebooks were outfitted with color-coded tabs, running well over a hundred pages.

The type of meeting determines to what extent documentation is needed and whether it needs to be bound in a notebook. When participants start getting confused with unnumbered papers flying around, it's time to organize and put documents into some type of binding.

 ## Step Four: Send the Meeting Invitation and Agenda

I was once the meeting chairman for a conference call and emailed all the scheduling information, agenda, and supporting documents to the meeting participants ahead of time. However, one person never joined the call. After the meeting, I called him to find out what happened. "Oh," he said, "I never received notice there was a meeting." Sure enough, his email address was missing from the list. It was a simple mistake, but it emphasizes how important an invitation is. If a formal meeting invitation isn't part of your company's procedures or if the meeting will include participants who don't typically attend, be sure to get a confirmation the invitation was received.

Decide when the invitation, agenda, and supporting documents will be sent. This time frame should be chosen depending on the type of meeting and the volume of content. Be consistent with delivering it on time, setting the standard for recurring meetings. This deadline should leave time for everyone to read and prepare. Establish a ground rule that all participants will have read the agenda and supporting documents before walking into the meeting. The key is to avoid the situation in which someone walks in scrambling to pull together documents or is ill-prepared to discuss the topic. One exception would be when the presenter wants a first-impressions response to a subject.

 ## Step Five: Prepare the Participants and Meeting Space

When it came time to prepare for one of the most important meetings of the New Testament, Jesus said to Peter and John, "Go and prepare the Passover for us, that we may

eat it." They asked, "Where will you have us prepare it?" (Luke 22:8–9). Jesus described how they would meet a man who would show them an upper room furnished and ready for them to prepare the Passover. "And they went and found it just as he had told them, and they prepared the Passover" (Luke 22:13). While not every meeting is as high stakes as the intimate gathering of Jesus and His disciples before His death, the practical details that go into preparing spaces can be thoughtfully crafted to align with the purpose of the meeting.

Several questions should be answered when preparing the participants and space for the meeting:

Are additional conversations needed to prepare participants for the discussion? Serving leaders do not want their people to be caught flat-footed in a meeting. Certain types of meetings or sensitive discussions are most successful when participants are given a heads-up to specific details. For example, if there will be layoffs, disclose this information privately to the individuals affected before announcing it in a meeting of the whole company.

Illustration 4: Serving leaders custom design their preparation to best serve each type of meeting.

Some participants can lend their support on a decision or idea if given more time to think about it before having to weigh in. For example, asking a board member to support an idea being brought to the table can facilitate a discussion that makes a decision more efficiently.

Is your meeting space ready? What meeting resources or equipment are needed in your meeting room? Consider the lighting, temperature, and refreshments. Do you need a projector, extension cord, whiteboard, markers, batteries, or large Post-it® stand with paper? What about the seating? Is the room arranged with productivity and engagement in mind?

Little structure may work at times for small companies, but for more advanced organizations, structure is necessary in every phase of the meeting. It's to your advantage to custom design your meeting preparation to fit each specific type of meeting used in your organization (see illustration 4).

Here are key indicators you're *not* prepared for a meeting:

- unvetted agenda items creeping in and stealing valuable meeting time
- failure to adequately research and prepare for an important agenda item
- disorganized documents
- rush to send last-minute agendas and scheduling reminders
- a meeting room without the necessary equipment

Leading the Meeting

In this chapter, we're discussing only the structure of leading the meeting. Leading includes facilitation, engagement, synergy, and ownership, all of which will be addressed in chapters 4–7. Several fundamentals to leading a structured meeting include establishing ground rules, delegating note-taking, and leading the agenda (see illustration 5).

Establish Ground Rules

Establishing ground rules or guardrails for your meeting will protect your team from needless inefficiencies and issues. These ground rules need to be decided by the group and followed by all. How much distraction is allowed? Can people use their electronic devices during the meeting? Agree on your team's level of focus and attention that everyone commits to, which ushers in the possibility of great engagement. If the meeting is virtual, does your team have online etiquette? How does the team handle people showing up late? What's the rule of thumb if someone isn't ready for their discussion point? What's the expectation of preparedness for all attendees?

Illustration 5: A serving leader leads the meeting by establishing ground rules, delegating note-taking, and leading the agenda.

The answers to these questions and more will set the tone for your team's meeting culture and productivity.

Delegate Note-Taking

As mentioned in the preparation stage, the person taking notes should not be the same person leading the meeting. This ensures freedom on the part of the serving leader to focus on facilitation and leadership.

Note-taking increases clarity for everyone, regardless of the sharpness of a person's memory. Good notes result in accurate information about (1) what actions are to be completed by what deadline and (2) what decisions were made. Notes capture wisdom and empower the person responsible to act with bold confidence and in sync with other participants who hold a stake in the action. If good notes are taken for a meeting, misunderstanding of what was discussed, decided, or committed to goes to near zero.

More importantly, meeting notes enable the meeting leader to participate in multiple meetings throughout the day without needing a photographic memory to retain volumes of information. Without recorded notes, a leader can quickly hit the ceiling of mental capacity and drop the proverbial ball.

Meeting notes are not transcripts of the meeting. Concise summary comments are best. When reread prior to the next meeting, great notes will remind a serving leader of the relevant details of a discussion.

It's often best if the meeting notes are recorded directly under each discussion point.

When taking notes, keep in mind these four potential end points for each item:

1. an understanding
2. a decision
3. a to-do
4. a tabled item

Imagine if the disciples had forgone recording what Jesus said and did? We wouldn't have insight into Jesus's life on earth without this important task. These records bring us understanding to questions the crowds asked, decisions Jesus made, instructions He outlined for those who followed Him, and even topics He deferred because it wasn't the right time.

> " **Notes capture wisdom and empower the person responsible to act with bold confidence and in sync with other participants who hold a stake in the action.** "

From a structural standpoint, I find it helpful to lead meetings from an outcome perspective. What type of outcome or result is needed with a point on the agenda? At the most basic level, an item will result in either an understanding, a decision, or a to-do. Most decisions or to-dos need an understanding to occur prior to making a decision or assigning a task.

An Understanding

Some discussions result in a mental understanding important to everyone. This includes issues like general knowledge of events, schedules, facts, happenings, feelings, or a perspective shared in the meeting. Such knowledge or information informs or educates the participants, but no direct action needs to be taken.

For example, most reports are an understanding, such as a financial report or a key performance indicator (KPI) report. Even personal tidbits shared at the beginning of a meeting are a type of understanding. Presenting information, solving problems, and making plans are all essentially forming understandings as a group.

Leading toward an understanding often results in a sort of mini policy (a way of thinking or seeing), and a good notetaker captures the understanding in a summary statement.

A Decision

Some topics about a situation, a problem, or an opportunity naturally lead to a decision. As stated above, a good understanding of the issues often precedes a decision. Before making a decision, it can be helpful to have the secretary verbally summarize to ensure everyone understands the decision on the table. In note-taking, if the decision was the main reason for the discussion, the preceding understandings may not need to be noted, only the final decision.

Consider whether you want your decisions to be highlighted in the notes. For example, color-coding, bolding, underlining, or italicizing helps reviewers quickly see the decision points.

A To-Do

I consider to-dos to be the most important part of note-taking. Yet for many years of leading meetings, I didn't include to-dos in meeting notes. When recording to-dos or action items, use this simple but powerful procedure:

First, make sure a name is assigned to each one. If a person has more than one to-do, group them together so their set of to-dos are next to each other for quick reference.

Second, write the to-do using a verb to describe the sort of action to be taken, and use adjectives or nouns to describe what's acted upon.

Third, always include a deadline. For example, instead of "decision about new distributor," write the action to be taken as, "Email Steve contact information of new distributor by end of day Friday and notify sales team at Monday's meeting." In short, to-dos should include who does what by when.

Finally, I suggest highlighting the to-dos or assignments by listing them separately near the bottom of the notes. By grouping the list of assignments in one place, it enables participants to quickly scan the list at the end of the meeting or at a later time.

A Tabled Item

During discussions, there can be many reasons for a topic to get postponed to another meeting. Sometimes more information is needed for further discussion, or the group ran out of time. Keep track of all tabled items in a "parking lot" in the notes for future meetings. This list of items can be referred to during the preparation stage of the next meeting or added to the agenda of an already scheduled meeting.

Often the last question I ask in a meeting is: "Did anything come up in our meeting that we should list as a tabled item for next meeting?"

Lead the Agenda

The following list outlines different phases or subphases of meetings. These phases may not be present in every meeting and often vary widely depending on the type of meeting you're leading. For example, a meeting focused solely on making one big decision may not contain much news, nor will such a meeting likely contain reporting. But for a weekly

management meeting, or even a board governance meeting, most of these phases will apply:

Welcome

- getting present
- personal connection

News

Reports

- financials
- KPIs
- goals
- to-dos

Discussion

- presenting
- brainstorming
- planning
- problem-solving
- decision-making

Wrap-Up

Welcome

Nothing is so obvious—and at the same time seemingly small—as the starting time for a meeting. As a serving leader, serve your followers by setting the standard—and living by it—of starting and being on time yourself. A foundational, timely start to a meeting can make or break things that come later, like engagement and synergy.

Getting Present: If you want to pave the way to relationally rich and people-centric meetings, start with the disciplines of focus and presence.

Focus emphasizes the importance of mental alertness and energy and the discipline to stay centered around the people and content of the meeting. By contrast, indulging in distractions will be detrimental. For any participant—but *especially* for the leader—wandering thoughts are the great enemies of focus. At Seven Oaks Landscaping, my friend David Bower's business in Virginia, the leader of their weekly management meeting welcomes the team by reading their vision, mission, and core values. While unique, this way of opening the meeting focuses the team. They believe it doesn't serve their company to be making decisions without being reminded of their core values and the reason they have for existing.

After shifting attention away from all mental distractions, engage with your heart and body. As Jim Elliot put it, "Wherever you are, be all there." Do a quick check-in with your heart to determine if you're fully present. Do you want to be in the meeting? Acknowledging how you are feeling can pave the way so you can put your heart on the table (see illustration 6).

For a brief heart check to occur, leaders can open meetings by inviting partic- ipants to express heartfelt concerns and desires. As a serving leader, your heart determines the meeting culture. It's your choice to use an "all business, no chitchat" approach, or to create space and time for people to bring their whole being. Just as sitting down to enjoy the nourishment of a good meal deserves a moment of silence or prayer, so too, good meetings can start by orienting and connecting our hearts with the Lord and each other.

Illustration 6: A serving leader brings their heart to the meeting by showing up fully present.

Personal Connection: When I met with Elam Esh to witness how they ran their meetings, I noticed the meeting room had the most unusual conference table I'd ever seen. It was a bar-height table with barstools around the perimeter. At first, I was a little taken aback. I expected to see cushy leather executive chairs, comfortable and easy to settle into. As I pondered the idea of spending the whole day at this bar-height conference table in stools without seat backs, Elam must have read my mind.

The first thing he taught me about meetings was that posture matters. They found when they used barstools around the table, people leaned for- ward. With this change in body posture, they became more focused, attentive, and engaged. "We believe in looking each other in the eye," Elam said. "And we believe in literally leaning into the meeting."

To make his point, Elam held eye contact with me until I got uncomfortable. Elam had

me hooked. I was all-in to learning about his meeting culture.

I was impressed at what a mastermind Elam was on meeting structure, even down to the configuration of his meeting room. He handed me a bottled water on the end of the table.

> " **Connect with others through eye contact and an attitude that says, 'I'm glad to be with you.'** "

"Thirsty?" I'd just traveled for several hours and hadn't thought about it, but I was thirsty. "Thank you," I said.

Elam smiled a knowing grin. "Your body matters in a meeting. Water is one of the fuels that keep you firing on all cylin- ders. You'll notice, I'm not serving you sugary drinks. I want people to have what they need to bring 100 percent to the meeting."

As I twisted the cap off the water bottle, Elam continued, "We also make a big deal about connecting at the beginning of meetings, not just face-to-face eye contact, but heart-to-heart contact. We're not all business around here. We start our meeting with a prayer and a psalm." He went on to elaborate on why human connection matters in meetings. "If people don't bring their desire, emotions, and values to the meeting, a large part of them is missing."

In the day of virtual meetings and electronic devices, the old-fashioned experience of face-to-face connection has become less frequent. Connect with others through eye contact and an attitude that says, "I'm glad to be with you." Use the first few minutes of the meeting to welcome each person with individual acknowledgment, if possible. Opening with "Thank you for joining us," or "It's good to be together," are examples of ways to welcome people. Create an atmosphere that allows those you lead to feel a sense of delight that your relationship with them is of paramount importance, more valuable than even the content of the meeting itself.

Depending on what brings people together for a meeting, the way connection happens can vary. Some leaders use team-building activities. Others share a win from the week. A one-on-one meeting with a colleague may take an unstructured approach and simply be a few minutes of catching up.

No matter what method you use to bring your team together to connect personally, this relational foundation strengthens the team for what's to come. Hard discussions are easier when there's connection before the tough moments. Knowing more about each other can create additional pathways for empathy or understanding.

News

This phase of the meeting is used to share highlights about what's important to your team culture. The key is sharing bite-size

> " Leaders who fail to regularly affirm and celebrate when a team member demonstrates company values are leaving cultural formation up to chance. "

points (less than one minute) that will help participants stay in tune with each other's areas of work. This will take discipline to practice, and you must recognize the difference between a small tidbit of news and a discussion point. Patrick Lencioni calls these small tidbits "lightning flash" reports. They illuminate a point of interest quickly (in a flash). Examples of news include employee or customer stories, event information such as an upcoming vacation, or quick updates. It can also include the key tasks of a person's week or a positive highlight relevant to the group.

Most importantly, this is the time to tell brief stories or testimonies about people who are living out the company's core values. When we verbally acknowledge someone and express gratitude, it becomes much easier for them to connect to the company's great purpose. This is a powerful way to reinforce what your company stands for. Leaders who fail to regularly affirm and celebrate when a team member demonstrates company values are leaving cultural formation up to chance.

Reports

Keep this stage of the meeting brief. Again, this is not the time for discussion. Separate reporting and discussion as much as possible to increase productivity and effective time management.

This takes discipline. If something reported requires discussion, determine if it should be moved into the discussion phase of the meeting. Separating reporting from discussion helps participants manage the mental load of listening and absorbing information, saving most of their brain power for the discussion.

There are four types of reporting to consider when structuring this phase of the meeting.

Financial Reports: When thinking about reports, financial reports quickly come to mind—and for good reason. Financial reports are history, and they reveal the score on many fronts. Financial numbers show trend lines that, while historical, are still good indicators for where the company is headed. Many great discussions are sparked because of the startling truth of these numbers.

KPI Reports: Key performance indicators will paint a vivid picture of the company's current operations. As such, indicators should be leading, not lagging, and bring early identification of potential problems. Not surprisingly, some small organizations don't track KPIs because leaders are working side-by-side with their team each day and already have insight into daily operations and performance. However, even small organizations will benefit from tracking and reporting on leading KPIs.

For Elam's furniture company with forty-five employees, the "scorecard" (as he called his KPI tracker) was critical. Elam pulled out a set of 3x5 weekly scorecards from his shirt pocket and dropped them onto the table. They were printed in full color with numbers and graphs on both sides of the card. "This scorecard is our company pulse," Elam said with an air of seriousness. "Every week a new set of numbers and graphs are printed on these 3x5 cards, and all the managers get a scorecard. We carry them around in our shirt pockets because it indicates the performance standard to which we are all accountable. If any of the KPIs are off track, we talk about it. This piece of the meeting is one of our most powerful reporting tools. In one minute, I have a snapshot of our entire operation."

Goals Reports: Track your goals through reporting to determine your trajectory. In annual strategic planning meetings, you'll want to review long-range goals, generally three to five years out. In quarterly meetings, review if you're on track to hit your annual goals. In weekly meetings, review your progress toward your quarterly goals. It can be helpful to report whether you or your team is on-track for the goal or off track. Off track goals can then be further discussed to course correct.

To-Do Reports: This type of reporting fits well into recurring meetings, at which participants are given assignments to be completed by the next meeting. Reporting on progress and completion of assignments and to-dos is one of the most effective methods to drive performance. Reporting on to-dos enables a person to give account of their progress, which creates a feeling of accomplishment. Even when a to-do isn't completed, written to-dos provide accountability and transparency.

If an extended discussion is needed about an incomplete to-do or about a difficulty encountered, move it to the discussion portion of the meeting.

Use check boxes in front of each written to-do as a place to indicate completion. If all the boxes are checked, everyone knows with a glance that the to-dos are completed.

By including a clear list of to-dos, assignments, and follow-ups during your meetings, there's less burden to hold people accountable outside of meetings. Plus, the group accountability helps emphasize how each member is an instrumental part of the team.

In summary, don't report on things for reporting's sake. Here's the acid test: If something needs attention or improvement, it's worth measuring and reporting.

Discussion

This is the meat of the meeting, and the largest segment. It may contain one item (in a single-focus meeting) or multiple subphases, depending on the type. If the news or report phase introduced any additional discussion topics, address them here. Also consider if any last-minute topics should be added. Consider the best place to insert new discussion points using the same decision-making process used to set the agenda.

You can also prioritize the discussion points as a group and list the most important topics first. Place items last that can be feasibly bumped to the next meeting if time runs out. Reorder the discussion points so the sequence creates a logical flow of information or discussion if new points were added.

Presenting: Presentations are often structured with sharing information first, then a time for questions and group discussion afterwards. Remember, visual aids can greatly enhance the understanding of your content.

Brainstorming: During discussion, there's often a need for a new idea or solution. Set attendees up for a win by beginning with vital information, such as any relevant restraints to ideas or how the idea will be used in the end. For example, you wouldn't want your team coming up with a great idea that would never fit in the budget, so if there's a financial constraint, begin by disclosing the boundaries before brainstorming begins.

Consider an exercise to get the creative juices flowing. For example, having the group throw the worst ideas onto the table can create some laughs and set the stage for fresh brainstorming. Refrain from reacting to ideas you don't initially like until all ideas are on the table. Once brainstorming has wound down, lead the team to choose top ideas, and potentially chart a path toward how the ideas could be used.

Planning: When planning, begin with clarity around the goal of the discussion, how much planning is needed, and the desired result. Any rough framework or pieces of the plan that are known or already decided should be disclosed. Consider the meeting Nehemiah had with King Artaxerxes when he requested to be sent to Judah to rebuild the city (Nehemiah 2:5–8). There were countless details that went into rebuilding the walls of Jerusalem. Leading the team includes guiding brainstorming (which results in vision for what the accomplishment of a plan could look like) and filling in details. Don't forget to review the completed plan with your team and confirm what needs to happen next.

> " **Truly understanding the problem that needs to be solved is essential before jumping into potential solutions.** "

Problem-Solving: Lead your team's problem-solving efforts by beginning with exploring the facts prior to a meeting discussion. Carefully research at the scene with the people involved. Clarify and break down the problem. Hold experiments and collect data to confirm all assumptions. Problem-solving is rarely possible in a meeting away from the site where the problem occurred. As such, truly understanding the problem that needs to be solved is essential before jumping into potential solutions. Make sure you and the group are clear on what type of solution is needed, or if there are constraints the solution must fit into, such as limits your company has around time, resources, or commitments.

Remember, you as the leader are responsible for the psychological safety present or absent at the table. Dig to the root of the problem, navigating away from things like blame and other unproductive discussion (see illustration 7). Be aware that sometimes an issue needs another venue—for example, a sensitive issue needing a private meeting or maybe a topic simply needing further research to be fully understood.

Lead the team through discussing pros and cons, and drive toward an action plan that includes accountability and follow-up.

Decision-Making: When leading toward decisions, it helps if surrounding information is presented beforehand, such as relevant facts, research, pros and cons, and risk factors. Is all the necessary information on the table to make this decision? Has your team had enough time to discuss? What does the process look like for a group to reach a decision, or is there someone who has the final say? As a serving leader, your team is best served by someone who drives toward action while drawing out the individual voices around the table. Once a decision is reached, determine if a specific to-do needs to be assigned.

Illustration 7: A serving leader digs to the root of the problem, exposing the root cause with love.

Wrap-Up

All meetings are brought to an effective close through summary. Like any speaking engagement, tell your audience what you will tell them, then tell them, and then tell them what you told them. This will vary from meeting to meeting, but typically a wrap-up will include up to four points. Someone should be responsible for watching the time, and provide a five- to ten-minute heads-up prior to the meeting end time.

In the wrap-up, begin by reviewing the list of to-dos and assignments from the meeting. Do this verbally or visually. It's critical to denote the deadline for each assignment. Secure commitments from each person who'll be accountable for a to-do, and lock in a common understanding of exactly what's expected and by when.

Second, review any discussion items in the current meeting that were tabled for the next meeting, as well as new items that emerged and are slated for future discussion.

Third, ask whether any information discussed needs to be communicated to anyone who wasn't present. If so, assign someone to relay the information.

Fourth, consider reflecting on what went right or consider how you could improve on the meeting in the future. This could look like going around the room and giving a number between one and ten. If an aspect of the meeting was difficult, consider asking for feedback. Don't hide trouble. Admit it and confess it. Champion better meetings by pointing out and valuing good meeting behaviors and attitudes.

Elam's company made a big deal about reflecting on and evaluating their meetings. Still sitting on my backless barstool, I listened as Elam elaborated on how they wrap up their meetings. "We shoot for Level 10 meetings," he said. "I got the term from Geno Wickman's *Traction* book. Around here, we measure what's important to us. What you measure tends to improve, so at the end of every meeting, we score our meetings on a scale of 1–10." He pulled another 3x5 card from his pocket and slid it across the table. On the right side of the card were five meeting qualities. Next to the meeting descriptions were weekly columns reflecting the rating of their meeting scores.

I stared at the card, a bit surprised. "Are you serious? You actually score your meetings?"

Elam answered, "We don't call them Level 10 meetings for no reason. Leaders like myself tend to overrate meetings. These cards tell the real truth—from the participants."

Finally, wrap up the meeting on time. Starting and ending on time is a critical part of meeting structure. This skill of punctuality is not accomplished by merely abruptly ending the conversation. Rather, like an airplane on approach to the runway, a serving leader must carefully manage the meeting airspeed for a smooth and final landing.

Here are key indicators a meeting phase was *not* led properly:

Welcome

- lack of eye contact, heart connection, or warmth
- insufficient connection time to chitchat and catch up
- distractions from personal electronics and communications
- late arrivals

News

- news that isn't short and succinct
- information that isn't relevant to others
- lack of celebrating core values shared through stories

Reports

- lack of accountability from the previous meeting's assignments
- poor quality or irrelevant information shared in reports
- lack of discipline to keep reporting on topic

Discussion

- poor or awkward transitions between subphases of the meeting
- agenda items poorly organized, sequenced, and prioritized
- presentations that are ill-prepared, haphazard, or aimless, leading to few if any conclusions or decisions
- discussions veering off topic without timely course correction
- poor time management, causing important topics to get pushed to a subsequent meeting

Wrap-Up

- lack of review of the to-do list
- incomplete communication of relevant content to parties absent from the meeting

Following Up after the Meeting

All's well that ends well, as Shakespeare put it, but a great meeting with weak follow-through is disappointing at best, and leads to failed projects, missed deadlines, and interpersonal conflict at worst. Great follow-up begins with serving leaders having the mindset that meetings are the hub—the center which drives action. Because meetings contain the collective strength of insight and direction of the group, it is imperative there is follow-through on understandings, decisions, and to-dos.

 Step One: Publish Meeting Notes

There is an art to taking good notes. Great note-takers capture 90 percent or more of the action. Quality notes, when read a week or even a month later, should trigger one's memory to recall the central themes of the meeting. Before publishing meeting notes, edit them. Consider one final read-through, then send them out within one day of the meeting or whatever standard is set. Store meeting notes and assignments where everyone can access them easily. Consider online platforms so participants can return to the notes later. For example, you could use OneNote or the Asana® collaboration work management platform. This will make adding afterthoughts to the tabled items simple.

Step Two: Reflect on the Meeting

Meeting notes are not for the dustbin. They're recorded so thorough review and reflection is possible. This is especially mind-freeing for leaders who pass in and out of many meetings per week. With good meeting notes, there's no worry about forgetting important commitments, concepts, and decisions.

Sometimes the best ideas come to you after the meeting. Our minds often innovate during silent contemplation, after being stimulated by spirited discussion. Richard Branson said, "If you don't write your ideas down, they could leave your head before you even leave the room." If afterthoughts merit further group discussion, capture your inspirations and add them to the parking lot (tabled items) of the meeting.

Consider making a habit of reviewing meeting notes for five to ten minutes after the meeting, or if recurring, several days prior to the next meeting. Consider a structured calendar event where meeting reflection is done.

First, reflect on your own performance and leadership during a meeting. As the meeting leader, a critical point of ownership is considering improving upon your own meeting skills. Humbly reflecting on a weakness or failure, however small, can lead to transformation. But also, don't forget to reflect on your strengths to further leverage and utilize them.

Second, reflect on the other participants' responses, and determine whether anything merits further comments or discussion. I was once in a meeting where agreement could not be reached, and the leader navigated the differences, which eventually ended in a 3–2 vote. Several days later, even though I had been in the minority during the vote, I felt gratitude toward that leader for how graciously and forthrightly he led that difficult discussion. I emailed and commended him for his even-handed approach. In a similar vein, consider whether anything that surfaced in the meeting warrants a one-on-one conversation. What's said or not said (nonverbal language) in a group meeting is sometimes a critical point to pick up on later when you're alone together. In this sense, without carving out time to reflect, the full crop of a meeting may not be harvested.

Third, reflect on things you observed in the meeting. These observations are as important as the discussion itself. Look for hints of truth or feelings that weren't fully expressed or were not appropriate to bring up in a group setting. Reflect on clues to emotional stress or strong feelings that were evident. These sorts of observations can be further explored in one-on-one meetings, if needed. To ensure follow-up on such an observation, write a reminder directly in the notes section of your next one-on-one meeting with that person. The bridge between topics discussed in group meetings and one-on-ones should be well-worn.

Here's a typical question I use to link an observation in a group meeting to a one-on-one meeting: "Do you want to talk more about this issue?" Or "If I read you correctly, you seemed troubled and uncertain about this. Could you say more?" Use reflection to identify and deal with a problem that surfaced but didn't belong in the group meeting. To be clear, I'm not suggesting having a talk with someone because you didn't have the discipline to talk about it around the meeting table, but rather that these types of conversations take place at the proper time within regularly scheduled one-on-one meetings.

> " Our minds often innovate during silent contemplation, after being stimulated by spirited discussion. "

When you observe a positive meeting behavior in a group setting, consider pointing it out. This can be a way to powerfully mentor meeting skills under your management. You can also jot down a note to compliment in private. When following up on such observations, participants feel understood and encouraged. More importantly, they feel your commitment to life-giving meetings through your actions.

Step Three: Complete To-Dos

As a serving leader, demonstrate accountability and credibility by completing your own assignments. This simple but profound discipline came from the coaching Ray provided to us at AgSalt. During the season of relearning how to improve my meetings, this practice became a game changer. For years, I had facilitated meetings assuming everyone could keep to-dos in their heads. This was a crazy assumption because I was one of the first to forget, yet I was stubbornly stuck in the habit of leading meetings without tracking tasks. Regularly, I ended meetings without even verbally recounting the to-dos to verify everyone was clear on their particular action item. Not surprisingly, many agreed upon tasks were forgotten, only to resurface as a failure in project completion later. Completing to-dos may feel like a tiny thing, but it is one of the most powerful disciplines in driving task-related performance.

> " The company that follows through on its weekly to-dos is the only company that will accomplish its annual goals. "

Set the example by demonstrating regular follow-through of to-dos. Discuss from time to time the percentage rate of completed to-dos, and push for an 80–90 percent completion rate or whatever standard you decide. The company that follows through on its weekly to-dos is the only company that will accomplish its annual goals. Track your weekly execution of tasks to yield results, and it just might put you in front of your competition.

Here are key indicators of poor meeting follow-up:

- no published meeting notes or hard-to-find records
- no dedicated place to record ideas that strike after the meeting
- no time set aside to reflect on meetings
- to-do completion rate of under 80 percent

Chapter Four

Meeting Facilitation

In a good meeting there is a momentum that comes from the spontaneous exchange of fresh ideas and produces extraordinary results. That momentum depends on the freedom permitted the participants.

HAROLD GENEEN

Meetings often are weak because leaders lack understanding and skill in how to facilitate. A meeting can be well-structured with a great agenda, and still stumble due to poor facilitation. The role of the facilitator is to design the approach taken in a discussion or presentation. Simply talking your way through the meeting's agenda is not facilitating. Instead, skillful facilitators move through the agenda tailoring the most effective approach for each agenda item.

More importantly, facilitation is about paying attention to the people in the room and drawing out their best contributions. As Kevin Hoffman writes in *Meeting Design*, "The facilitator is a balancing force, keeping contributions equal and fair."[6] Ultimately, facilitators must learn to manage the power and influence in the room.

Here are five areas of facilitation:

1. meeting flow
2. visual aids
3. questions
4. contribution
5. conflict

Facilitating Meeting Flow

The term *meeting flow* is borrowed from the ebb and flow of tidal waters. When the tide goes out and recedes, it ebbs; when it comes back in, it flows. Ebb is a state of departure, decline, or decay. In relationships, ebbing can mean less connection or relational distance.

Meeting flow is when a meeting is moving along nicely, versus haltingly. It's making progress versus circling or being stuck.

Meeting flow contains three concepts: time management, staying on topic, and summarizing or drawing a conclusion of an understanding, a decision, or a to-do.

Meeting ebb and decline involve poor time management, rabbit trailing off topic, and failure to draw the tangled threads of a discussion to a conclusion.

In a nonprofit board meeting, the chairperson and vice chairperson are responsible for meeting flow. On management teams, often the meeting leader and notetaker are the best pair to guide the conversation.

Time Management

Skillful facilitators watch the clock. Time management matters throughout the whole meeting, but especially during discussions. Here are three pointers that will help maximize the use of your time.

First, in preparing for the meeting, every discussion item should be delegated to someone who comes ready to present the issue. Without thinking through the issues ahead of time, meandering presentations abound. Teach your participants to make their presentations clear and succinct.

Second, maintain time-awareness during discussion. A wall clock that all participants see can be helpful, but nothing's more effective than the leader pointing out the time at intervals throughout the meeting. It's okay to extend a discussion if necessary, but you must keep in mind the other important items on the agenda.

Consider timing the agenda and allocating specific amounts of time for each point. Time management isn't only about keeping things moving and timely; it's also about identifying when an issue needs more time. There's a place to stay with the issue and bump other items off the agenda so you can finish the discussion, but often it's necessary to make the choice to table it until a later meeting or designate a separate meeting for the topic.

> " Time management isn't only about keeping things moving and timely; it's also about identifying when an issue needs more time. "

Third, don't rush. I find time management is most difficult in the discussion phase. Rushing a discussion is not the silver bullet of time management. Issues need adequate time to be explained, for questions to be raised, and for alternative perspectives to be mixed in. The key is not racing the clock. It's moving the discussion along so the slowest thinker stays abreast but stretched. Be careful to slow down in order to dig a little deeper on a sticky problem, but be just as careful to move a dragging conversation along or to refocus a participant who goes off on a tangent.

Avoid long pauses by transitioning smoothly but quickly to the next person who needs to speak. Limit unnecessary questions that veer the discussion off course or into too much detail.

At AgSalt, Ray pushed me to use a timed agenda and a meeting timer that showed the time we had remaining on an issue. When the time expired, we forced ourselves to allocate five to ten minutes to finish the discussion. This may seem extreme, but it broke my bad habit of running meetings overtime.

Illustration 8:
Serving leaders guard against rabbit trails that could hijack the meeting.

Staying On Topic

Meeting flow includes staying on the meeting path. The agenda is the roadmap, but facilitators must establish the guardrails to keep the meeting in its lane. Staying on topic includes pulling the issue *back* when is strays off track, pulling it *down* when it drifts too high into the philosophical whys and wherefores, or pulling the issue *up* out of too much detail.

Pulling Back

Complex and interwoven issues tend to veer off into other important related issues as we seek to fully understand them, but rabbit trailing can easily be the result (see illustration 8). At Country Value Woodworks, they have a "bunny trail" bell anyone can ring when they believe the discussion is off track.

Sometimes the deviation down the trail turns up related information that will naturally lead back to the discussion. Using open-ended or closed-ended questions to explore a side trail can control the extent to which you explore. Regardless, maintain meeting flow by pulling the meeting back to the subject as soon as the related issue informs it. Little comments like, "That was helpful; now let's return to the topic with that in mind," can steer the meeting back on track.

Sometimes a rabbit trail leads to an issue relevant to the team but ultimately off topic. Because of its relevance or interest, the team keeps discussing it. A way to maintain the importance of such an issue is to put it on the list for another discussion so as not to lose it. But don't wait to table it until after it has hijacked the meeting.

Pulling Down

Unless the issue is strategic and overarching in nature, most issues don't need the thirty-thousand-foot view except for a brief moment. Zooming out can be helpful to link the issue to an overriding principle, core value, or strategic plan, but good meeting flow includes pulling the discussion back down to the practical and functional. The zoom-out isn't wasted as long as it informs and strengthens the discussion. Zooming out could look like reminding the group about a broad principle, such as your commitment level to team connection. In this example, the discussion should be brought back to how much time and energy the leadership team is willing to put into individuals to help them acclimate to the team.

Pulling Up

Good meeting flow includes enough detail to provide accurate information but not so much as to bury the group in minutiae. Be quick to redirect a conversation if it gets too detailed, or becomes unproductive. Often the felt need for sorting through details is rooted in the presenter's failure to prepare, to summarize the information, or to make the detailed information visual and scannable; therefore the group gets dragged through the weeds of too much information. A good facilitator can redirect such a meeting with a question like, "What point are you trying to make?"

Pulling It All Together

Sometime meetings drag on because no one pulls the discussion together in a timely manner. The nature of group discussion puts various perspectives and ideas on the table. But this can leave the group with unsorted pieces and parts that don't fit neatly together. "Where are we going with this?" must be on the leader's mind as a discussion progresses.

How do you bring this all together and tie the tangled threads into a knot? First, cut out the fluff—any misaligned or irrelevant information. Second, summarize what fits out of the overall conversation into concise, clear comments. Third, drive toward one of four results:

1. an understanding
2. a decision
3. a to-do
4. a tabling of the topic for a future meeting

Great facilitators keep the meeting flowing by pulling together the group's best contributions like puzzle pieces forming a complete picture.

Facilitating Through Visual Aids

Visual aids are the counterpart to verbal communication. Combining the visual with the verbal dramatically aids memory and understanding, and engages kinesthetic and visual learning with auditory learning, thus enhancing participation. Think about how easy it is to remember a person's face—and how easily we forget their name.

The simplest and most widely used form of visual aid is the printed meeting document or (in virtual meetings) an e-document of some sort. Once I was in a virtual meeting with a facilitator who used an Excel spreadsheet to show a complex concept and how a formula would work to calculate needed information. It would have been impossible for the participants to grasp the complexity of his idea without the visual aid of the spreadsheet.

A chart, graph, illustration, or drawing can convey in seconds what might take minutes to explain in words. As Kevin Hoffman points out in *Meeting Design*, "Concepts of time, connection, disconnection, emotion, and more can be represented more quickly with lines, boxes, arrows, and simple…drawings."[7] Illustrating an idea on a whiteboard with sketches enables an entire group to see the same thing, encouraging understanding and agreement.

A meeting with auditory words only, without the use of visual aids, can require exhausting levels of concentration. Visual aids pique interest, and people are usually more attentive to pictures, sketches, and diagrams, especially hand-drawn ones. It makes meetings more emotional and more human. Such visual communication styles connect people and reduce alienation while creating memorable moments.

Facilitating Through Questions

One of the best forms of engagement is asking great questions to further elicit and fill in gaps of knowledge. Nicodemus used questions when he engaged Christ while trying to understand the idea of being "born again." Struggling, he asked Jesus, "How can a man be born when he is old? Can he enter a second time into his mother's womb and be born?" (John 3:4). Like Nicodemus, ask questions to clarify confusing ideas or complex information. To simplify or move the discussion toward a shared understanding, use questions that are well thought out and provoking. These often reveal missing aspects of an issue and help reveal new angles and perspectives.

The power of questions is priceless, as they naturally invite participation. A good question at the right time can draw out excellent commentary, make room for new opinions, and inspire different insights. A good facilitator guides the direction of the issue with questions, while opening the floor for comments and sparking discussion.

Not all questions are equal. There are "proud" questions, and there are "humble" questions. Proud questions are the type that already contain an implied answer; the questioner is looking only for agreement. Such a question is typically asked while hinting the answer is already known. By comparison, humble questions are free of assumptions and honestly seek another perspective. The answer isn't implied or presumed. The best facilitators use humble questions to elicit discussion.

If you struggle with asking good questions, write out a list ahead of time, removing those with assumptions or implied answers.

Questions can be closed and focused, or open and broad. Both have their place. For example, at the beginning of a brainstorming session, open and broad questions will likely work well. Such questions spark creativity and help people think outside the box. On the other hand, after narrowing down various options in a discussion, more focused and closed-ended questions can help in reaching a conclusion.

Finally, design and use questions that explore different types of needed information, or to create an experience or mood. It takes vastly different inquiries to unpack the following five areas: facts, feelings, actions, motivations, and systems.

For example, if more facts are needed, you can ask, "What happened?" or "Could you describe that?" If feelings need to be explored, you can ask, "How do you feel about that?" If action or behavior needs addressing, you can ask, "Could you tell me what you did?" or "What steps did you take?" If motivation needs understanding, you can ask, "Why did this matter to you?" or "What do you want?" If exploring a system or a combination of factors, you can ask, "Could you link the related issues?" or "How does this relate to that?"

Questions, more than any other discussion tactic, help to draw out underlying assumptions, to expose gaps, and to tell the other side of the story.

Facilitating Contribution

Leading a meeting requires facilitating people's contributions and influence. Flow, visual aids,

and questions are important, but ultimately these three aspects of facilitation are in the service of the participants. In the end, the people around the meeting table need to be led. This includes helping them fully offer their contribution without unhealthy influence and power being wielded by a few, while others fall silent.

For the serving leader or facilitator, this means first restraining their own influence and drawing out others on an issue.

One time a leader opened an issue by stating his concluding opinion before inviting others to speak. It struck me as self-centered and a misuse of influence. It's one thing to serve others by framing up the issue with a few questions, options, or factors to get participants thinking. It's quite another to push directly for a decision or to leverage the group to one side of the issue before opening the discussion for fair discourse. Exercise oversight, "not domineering over those in your charge" (1 Peter 5:3).

Facilitating influence includes drawing out quieter members of the group, while requiring the highly vocal participants to be self-controlled. I remember a skilled facilitator kindly but firmly saying, "You've said your piece. It's time for others to voice their opinion." This was a necessary soft rebuke towards a highly knowledgeable individual who didn't know when to quit talking. Ultimately, facilitating discussions is about managing influence and relationships so the louder voices don't inadvertently become bullies and the timid souls don't lose their voice.

The personality of participants is always a factor in the level of verbal participation. Extroverts and domineering personalities always have more to say, but a good facilitator will take the precious few words of the quieter

> " Questions, more than any other discussion tactic, help to draw out underlying assumptions, to expose gaps, and to tell the other side of the story. "

participant and give it weight by highlighting it with a comment like, "Well said," or circling back to the comment later.

The meeting leader should be sensing the pulse of participants who may have something to contribute but who need to be drawn out by asking them to share. Watch facial expressions for clues of a desire to speak.

> " Offer your comments softly in the form of questions or with an air of humble consideration rather than bold assertion. "

In smaller meetings with only a few participants, you can expect everyone to respond to each issue. This isn't possible in larger meetings, however, so the meeting chairperson needs to be sharp and discern who has something to say, and whether what's being said is resonating with the broader group. This is something a perceptive leader can recognize as they study body language and facial expressions, such as the nod of the head and even subtle shifts in posture.

Managing the influence in the room doesn't mean equalizing influence, but it does mean knowing who the influence brokers are. Guard against any unintended domination that restricts the contribution of others, even if it comes from you.

Influential people need to limit their comments and listen when less influential people make their point. This requires self-regulation so other points of view can be fairly considered. Demonstrate humility and "count others more significant" than yourself (Philippians 2:3). The power broker in the room can easily become an unintentional bully. This is inevitable when individuals are highly skilled in knowledge of a complex subject but low in emotional intelligence. They typically spew their knowledge, overwhelming the group, and create low grades of fear so no one dares to counter their viewpoint. If you are one of the most influential in the room, don't leverage your words with forceful emotion and dramatic effect. Instead, offer your comments softly in the form of questions or with an air of humble consideration rather than bold assertion.

Facilitating Healthy Conflict

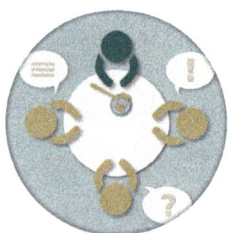

"When a group of intelligent people come together to talk about issues that matter," writes Patrick Lencioni in *Death by Meeting*, "it is both natural and productive for disagreement to occur."[8] Healthy discussion occurs when people are completely free to offer their perspective without fear. When people are at peace within themselves and not seeking to intimidate others, group members can contribute thoughts that enrich, complete, challenge, and stimulate further discussion.

This freedom to express one's perspective must be guarded by the meeting leader. I've witnessed countless times when meeting leaders allowed bullying, scorn, and passive aggression to derail or stymie the meeting. Gently and firmly call such participants to order.

This doesn't mean tough conversations are disallowed. To the contrary, in many cases honest disagreement and healthy conflict are the only way to turn up the heat enough to expose our differences and find the best path forward.

In Acts 15, the Jerusalem council used "much debate" (15:7) to work through their differences. Multiple people spoke up: Pharisees, Peter, Paul, Barnabas, and James. There may have been some facilitation because "all the assembly fell silent" (15:12) to allow Barnabas and Paul to speak. Finally, the person slowest to speak spoke up: James. He didn't start by voicing his own strong opinion, but rather quoted Peter, the Old Testament, and then Moses (15:13–21).

To create this culture of healthy conflict, participants must put their perspective on the table with full emotional engagement and without guarded walls of distance or a combative spirit. Participants are not going to be emotionally vulnerable in a disagreement, however, if the facilitator doesn't respect and value the truth that comes through emotion. A small word of encouragement can help people be honest, such as "I appreciate the depth of feelings behind your words," or acknowledge by saying "I sense the depth of your heart in that comment." We are people of desire and feelings. Even facts are sometimes emotionally loaded because we all want it to be true—even if it's false. Coming around and accepting someone else's perspective because yours was somewhat flawed is usually emotionally painful.

At the same time, be aware that disagreement brings the risk of people experiencing injury,

which tempts them to separate from each other. Even the Scriptures acknowledge the limit of disagreement: "Can two walk together, unless they are agreed?" (Amos 3:3, NKJV). But this principle does not mean we should quickly separate.

Because disagreements can be painful, especially for those who've been injured from past relationships (that's all of us), be on the lookout for participants who hide their opinions or disengage in the heat of debate and disagreement. Too many leaders are uncomfortable with conflict to the point they never get to the root of issues. They facilitate with an underlying motivation to avoid it. In such a meeting culture, the room too quickly goes silent or the issue is skirted—only to resurface at a later date or to remain buried forever. Instead, when conflict emerges, it should be viewed as a redemptive moment. Like the apostles, conflict requires coming together and considering the matter if it needs attention and resolution. Be a leader who enters into the uncomfortable, even excruciating pain of conflict.

Be aware that unresolved shame is sometimes buried in the heart of participants or facilitators, limiting the group's ability to fully enter into healthy conflict. Such a person refuses to be found on the wrong side of the issue and as such will either amp up their perspective to convince everyone they're right or bow out of the conversation and disengage emotionally. The latter is by far the go-to coping strategy in the world of Christian leaders that I know. A few take the route of being a bully supposedly standing for truth. But too many seek to calm the waves of conflict as quickly as possible while never resolving what is poisoning healthy debate. Be aware of people who insist on getting their own way by using rejection and aggression to silence others. Whether bullies win the conflict or people deny and disengage, both are death.

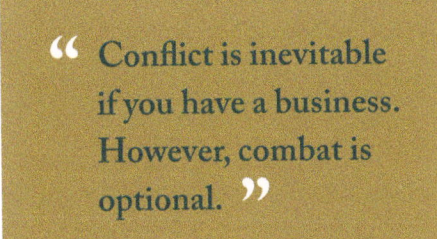

" **Conflict is inevitable if you have a business. However, combat is optional.** "

Negative feelings and attitudes like arrogance, superiority, and buried shame harm healthy debate.

As a facilitator, consider healthy silence as one of the key practices to use in disagreement. Silence is needed for a moment of truth to sink in. Slow down when the discussion gets tough, or pause the meeting for a brief break for quiet reflection. Keep in mind that issues can be tabled, allowing for a fresh look at a later date. "Let me sleep on it" is often a helpful response when the issue is deep and complex.

> " A dissenting opinion, while uncomfortable, is the test of the best and most important decisions and is very healthy for the organization. "

In disagreement, deep understanding is of upmost importance. Slow down the conversation and ask probing questions such as, "Say a little more" or "Could you further clarify that?" or give feedback to ensure clear understanding about what you hear them saying. When exploring differences, deepen the pool of meaning by questioning why those differences exist. Say, "I disagree, but here's why" or, "Let me explain another perspective." Never forget why the issue really matters. Dig deeper by asking, "Why does this difference exist?" Sometimes the difference is a philosophical or a strategic difference, but more often than not, it's a relational difference caused by repeated emotional injuries and attacks.

From my observation, participants far too often go silent to avoid the pain of disagreement just at the moment when such disagreement is needed most.

Wayne Wengerd, the founder of Pioneer Equipment, had this to say: "Conflict is inevitable if you have a business. However, combat is optional." At Pioneer, it's not uncommon for five or six different opinions to come up during a conversation. As a large family with twelve children, most of whom are stakeholders in the company, the Wengerds have found a way to interact without beating around the bush, even when it comes to the hard things. Daniel Wengerd, Wayne's son, said, "I like to call it healthy debate."

Healthy discussion weeds out the weak ideas and leads to the best decisions. To allow this, leaders need to "be quick to hear, slow to speak, slow to anger" (James 1:19). Listen until you can integrate others' perspectives, then build on what they say.

As Dwayne Borkholder once told me, "A dissenting opinion, while uncomfortable, is the test of the best and most important decisions and is very healthy for the organization." Dwayne Borkholder was one of the founding board members for Anabaptist Financial. He modeled and often offered a dissenting opinion. He did so with grace, never leveraging or manipulating others. Much of the content on healthy conflict in this guide I learned from observing Dwayne.

Here are key indicators of poor facilitation:

- discussions that often drift off topic
- verbal discussion with little visual aid to support it
- few questions asked
- loudest voice dominates the influence in the meeting
- meeting impacted by separation, silence, and passive aggression

Chapter Five
Meeting Engagement

*From whom the whole body, joined and held together
by every joint with which it is equipped.*

EPHESIANS 4:16

Meetings can be fulfilling and engaging. While this often isn't the reality for most, meetings should bolster a sense of oneness, synergy, and belonging.

Inwardly, everyone longs to belong—to be part of something bigger than themselves, something with a great purpose or cause. Meetings should make people feel alive! They should tap the innermost well of spiritual vitality, so life-giving engagement ensues from spiritual union with God. This is the source of meeting engagement. Meetings become deathlike because the spark of spiritual life is unkindled. In short, meeting engagement is showing up, fully present and on fire!

By contrast, disengaged participation happens when warm bodies show up with their inner human capacities turned off or distracted. As such, participants are disinterested, distracted, or distant, and the meeting lacks their rich contribution. Instead of being a fertile field for learning and listening, misunderstanding in the meeting is common. Instead of connection and camaraderie, coldness is felt. Instead of people sharing insights and perspectives safely, toxic conflict hangs in the air.

The real test of engagement in a meeting is whether the participants are all there—body, soul, and spirit.

Elements of Engagement

Human engagement is fully maximizing our capacities, talents, and senses to form connection and unleash potential. This includes intellectual horsepower, physical attentiveness, and spiritual vitality.

Intellectual

Intellectual engagement is what happens when a mind is focused, attentive, and processing. It includes being mentally alert, harnessing your brain power, and being aware of others. It's bringing your thoughts, knowledge, beliefs, and worldview with you. In the apostle Paul's words, "Take every thought captive to obey Christ" (2 Corinthians 10:5).

Physical

Being physically engaged in a meeting starts with bringing a healthy, rested body. Too often, we begin meetings with sugary drinks and donuts, then wonder why the meeting energy is low! Or we go from meeting to meeting, using caffeine as a crutch to prop up our energy levels. This is a vastly underrated problem in meetings. Along with healthy practices such as getting a good night's sleep and nourishing our bodies, physical engagement includes using good posture and eye contact. Coming ready for engagement can be demonstrated through our vitality for life and our expressiveness in conversation that draws people in. This is often accomplished through the practice of open and receptive body language.

Emotional and Spiritual

Emotional and spiritual engagement produces aliveness and connectedness around the table. It's using our spiritual discernment, intuition, conscience, and desires to engage others.

Meeting engagement is rooted or sourced in love, belonging, and connection. The power of love, like nothing else, draws out the full measure of human potential. When people feel they're valued, respected, and understood—all heaven breaks loose inside them. What ensues is a life-giving meeting, rich with engagement.

If hate is at the table, or any of its cousins—dislike, unhealed injuries between parties, or simply relational aloofness—engagement is cut off at the knees.

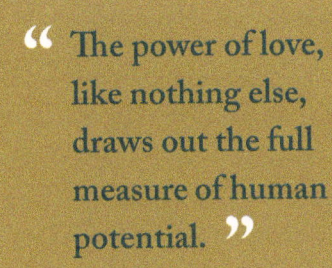

❝ The power of love, like nothing else, draws out the full measure of human potential. ❞

Active Listening

With love as the celestial air in the room, engagement is the art of listening, receiving, and absorbing information, values, and feelings. I call it "the listening posture." But we've all found ourselves disengaged and drifting off in a meeting.

A meeting shouldn't cause its listeners to fall out the window as Eutychus did in the book of Acts while Paul was preaching (Acts 20:7–12). However, listening and processing information can be tough, particularly after lunch, when the room is warm, you're short on sleep, and digesting a meal. Staying fully engaged and paying close attention requires the virtue of self-discipline.

Elam's backless barstools are a genius way to keep the body engaged—but I challenge you to stand up if you find yourself fading. While you're responsible to keep yourself steeled against internal distractions and in a receptive mental state, it's also incumbent on the speaker to remain engaging.

Staying engaged when you're required to be silent and receptive is a virtue for serving leaders to ascribe to. Steven Covey said it best: "Seek first to understand, then to be understood."[9] It's a matter of giving full respect and attention to understand the issues at hand.

The struggle of active listening escalates when the person speaking is poorly presenting. This is amplified when the content is difficult to absorb or isn't central to a participant's interest. However, sometimes paying attention requires us to endure in the same way we do when we sacrifice for the sake of another leader or department.

Nothing engages more than love flowing from the presenter with powerful facilitation tactics at play, making it easy for people to stay engaged.

The presenter should be self-aware and continuously evaluating by asking, "Am I engaging?

Is love flowing from me? Am I offering something logical, meaningful, and clear?" It's a good idea to pause periodically during a presentation, leaving space to ask those listening, "Are you following? Is this making sense? Any comments or questions?" A staple in presenting should include reinforcing one's topic with stories, which catch the listeners' attention while drawing them into deeper understanding.

Internal Processing

Active listening leads to internal processing. Engagement is being on fire "in the belly" as it were. Or to use an engine analogy, it's firing on all eight cylinders. Engagement is using all your capacities to fully process and internalize what's being presented (see illustration 9). This goes far beyond eliminating distractions and staying focused—which is like hitting a single and getting on base. Moving around the bases, though, requires processing information. This is often confirmed with the comment, "I'm following you." The intellectual work of internally processing facts, logic, and reason should lead to deep understanding and discernment, equipping the listener with the necessary information to move forward. To go one step further, full engagement allows for understanding the internalized values, underlying motives, and emotions of the presenter. In order for life-giving processing to occur, you must go beyond just intellectually understanding the discussion.

To achieve home run meetings full of engagement, leaders must help participants open up, become emotionally vulnerable, and fully experience the impact of the person speaking. Allow yourself to be moved by another's perspective. This doesn't mean becoming a pushover as a participant, someone who always says yes. Instead, it's being fully moved through internal processing (intellectually, emotionally, spiritually) to completely receive and understand someone's problem, viewpoint, wish, or desire. Such levels of meeting engagement set

Illustration 9: Serving leaders use their whole being to fully engage in the meeting.

the stage for vulnerability. Researcher and storyteller Brené Brown states, "Vulnerability is the birthplace of innovation, creativity, and change."

Such high engagement—if the heart is on fire—will often happen with open-ended questions or statements like these:

- "Say a little more about…"
- "Could you explain a little more…"
- "I need more clarification about…"
- "I understand what you're saying, but what are you *feeling* about this issue?"
- "Why does this issue matter to you?"

These kinds of comments lead to deeper understanding, which sets the team up for great synergy.

Here are key indicators of poor engagement:

- multiple distractions
- obvious or subtle disinterest displayed in listeners
- indifferent, closed off, or heavily guarded participants
- resistance to others' influence
- attendees sitting around the table with blank faces and eyes glazed over
- people who are tired, strung out on caffeine, or fighting sugar crashes or low blood sugar
- poor attention spans or people checking out during the conversation
- boring presentations that lack good questions and relevant stories

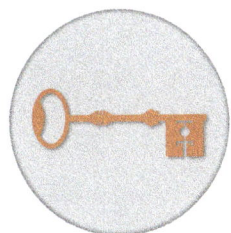

Chapter Six

Meeting Synergy

*Listening with our eyes and hearts, not just our ears
and brains, requires a deeper level of paying attention. It
requires that we listen for understanding and not for the words,
that we hear the heart and see the soul.*

JAMES KOUZES AND BARRY POSNER,
Encouraging the Heart

Synergy is when the pieces from multiple sources—such as feelings, ideas, and information—come together to form a whole. This whole is greater than the sum of its parts. In synergy, people build on each other by tapping into the power of combining complementary pieces.

> " **Instead of the high road of synergy, too many settle for meetings that subtly foster functional separateness.** "

Synergy is often the elusive X-factor of meetings. "Getting on the same page" is one of the modern expressions used to describe this synergistic phenomenon. In the Bible, Paul tells believers to be "eager to maintain the unity of the Spirit in the bond of peace. There is one body and one Spirit—just as you were called to the one hope that belongs to your call— one Lord, one faith, one baptism, one God and Father of all, who is over all and through all and in all" (Ephesians 4:3–6). In short, achieving oneness is synergy. But it takes "eagerness to keep the unity," (4:3) and even more effort to build that unity. Instead of the high road of synergy, too many settle for meetings that subtly foster functional separateness.

Elements of Synergy

Synergy utilizes the human capacity of mind, body, and spirit. These elements are hard-wired into our dignity or spirituality—the image of God.

Intellectual

Synergy is built with intellectual connections. A single idea or thought often needs to be linked to the next, then the next, until a whole or well-rounded conclusion emerges. Synergy is a meeting of the minds where multiple thoughts and perspectives come together in a powerful way. Synergy brings the best the participants have to offer and merges it into agreement.

Physical

Synergy is built through physical body language. A lot can be communicated in a meeting without saying a word. A nodding of the head indicates agreement; raising eyebrows with a smile communicates approval and eagerness to hear more; and creasing the forehead while narrowing the eyes can communicate thinking hard or processing. Cocking the head to the side can express a questioning thoughtfulness. These body languages cues are typically North American and may mean something else in other cultures.

Your posture speaks loudly in a meeting. Leaning forward communicates interest and desire to hear more. An erect posture denotes respect. Folding of the arms can indicate rejection or skepticism towards an idea, that the mind is already made up, or defensiveness.

Whether expressing consent or objection, the human body is a key player in building synergy with other participants while remaining silent.

Emotional and Spiritual

Synergy is built on shared desires, emotions, and feelings. Nothing transforms a meeting like connecting at a heart level. Understanding the presenter's feelings, not just their ideas, will create intuitive knowledge that can inform and move the meeting forward. It can be powerful to know a heart, its motives and desires, thus creating a link to better agreement, disagreement, or adjustment. Being "eager to maintain the unity" (Ephesians 4:3) includes the uniting of hearts.

Interpersonal Synergy

At an interpersonal level, synergy is being in tune with the feelings, emotions, and needs of other people in the meeting, thus creating a vibrant atmosphere. If a meeting is to be people-centric and life-giving, then the heart is certainly central to the meeting. Conversely, when a meeting is driven by a business and facts-only mindset, such meetings are lifeless, with hearts left in the hallway.

Synergistic meetings invite and foster heartfelt passion and emotional intelligence. Serving leaders recognize the place of true wisdom being found in the heart which expresses itself through feelings, desires, and intuition. As philosopher Blaise Pascal said, "The heart has its reasons, which reason does not know." Some people experience this through what they call a gut feeling or sense.

I'll never forget my surprise when, early in my leadership experience, I heard a chairman of a meeting during a high-stakes discussion caution the participants to "take emotions out of the decision." While well-intentioned, this leader assumed the best decisions are made without the heart. Desire and emotions should not over-shadow reason and facts, but instead be woven into the fabric of the meeting to achieve great decisions.

How then do participants foster interpersonal synergy?

Relational synergy must be valued as a meeting ideal and exemplified by the serving leader. Great meetings are first about knowing and being known: connection. To be sure, reports are necessary, discussions are needed, and decisions must be made. But unless such activities are grounded in a spirit of love and oneness, meetings can be mechanical and cold. Such connection is often expressed through facial expressions, tone of voice, and body language. These connection points are typically a nonverbal version of synergy that creates a life-giving atmosphere. Important signs of love, peace, pain, and fear are shared emotionally but often nonverbally.

Discussions become alive when participants synchronize themselves emotionally and spiritually. Some call this the "buzz" in the room or a sense of electrified human energy. A company that values a meeting culture rich with heart and passion will develop great synergy—great oneness (see illustration 10).

Synergistic Discussion

Synergistic discussion brings pieces of a puzzle together, linking thought to thought and comment to comment. It's positioning one perspective next to another to reveal the compatible features. These perspectives could be similar or quite different. In synergistic conversation, even seemingly divergent ideas are adjusted to find they fit together in a way that had seemed impossible.

Illustration 10: Serving leaders build momentum by drawing out participants' ideas and feelings.

Such synergistic discussions require adequate time to dive deep into the issues. Don't use most of the meeting time to present an issue and then expect deep synergistic discussion to occur in ten minutes. Beware of the well-intentioned presenter who's overconfident in their content and alienates participants with tightly clutched proposals rather than drawing participants in to wrestle with the hard questions and potential complications.

Putting the puzzle pieces together often requires multiple participants to lean into the discussion, all making their best arguments. Participants must value the pieces represented by others, and quite often must adjust their own to match.

This should never simply become a negotiation process that merely splits the difference. It isn't about who's right. Instead, through a rich exploration of possibilities, the best idea emerges. Synergy requires neither shrinking back nor asserting oneself but yielding, bending, and adapting while humbly submitting for the good of the whole. Such synergistic discussion occurs when it's aimed at a common goal and participants are committed to truth prevailing. However, people who speak the truth without love never achieve synergy. Instead, humility and love are the character traits that weave multiple perspectives together while discarding false or weak ideas—even when it's your own. The goal of synergy is to end up with a different but better answer together than what anyone could come up with alone. In this way, God "gives grace to the humble" (James 4:6).

When Pioneer Equipment brought business consultants in to help them improve their discussions, the consultants helped the brothers realize they had to go beyond their own stand-alone ideas. Even if an original idea was a great one, they learned it must be beat up and forged in the heat of healthy debate. Like the blows of a hammer on heated metal, a collective idea is a better idea, reshaped on the anvil of synergy.

Rarely is one person's perspective well-rounded. And it's equally as rare an idea falls from heaven fully developed. If a discussion is dominated by the

> **" Synergy requires neither shrinking back nor asserting oneself but yielding, bending, and adapting while humbly submitting for the good of the whole. "**

loudest voice or by the most influential voice, the participants will fall short of the goal of a shared perspective. The key to unlocking synergistic meetings is to first repent of and transform character flaws of arrogance (when more knowledgeable than others), unyieldedness, and self-interest. "Beloved, I urge you as sojourners and exiles to abstain from the passions of the flesh, which wage war against your soul" (1 Peter 2:11). Flawed character and desires wage war against meetings. By comparison, the discipline of synergy is working together to harness the collective strength of the group. Two horses together can pull three times the weight that a single horse can pull alone; this is the law of synergy.

Here are key indicators of a lack of synergy:

- hearts and feelings left out of the meeting, emotionally crippling the conversation
- pushing an agenda instead of inviting other ideas or perspectives
- dominant personalities that silence good discussion
- ignoring gut feelings and intuitive knowledge that crop up during discussion

Chapter Seven

Meeting Ownership

Everything you do in a meeting is a choice and will have an impact, and conscientious people pay attention to the impact they are having on others.

J. ELISE KEITH, *Where the Action Is*

When it comes to meetings, ownership is about humbly taking responsibility. It means accepting the weight of mistakes, stumbling, and weaknesses. It's the attitude of "How can I help?" that lifts the meeting to high altitude. Ownership carries the torch of culture into the meeting with its shining values of truth and goodness.

Take Responsibility

Who is responsible for the meeting? At first thought, most will assume it's the leader. In the ultimate sense, that's true. But let's push the bar of responsibility one notch higher. What if the meeting were owned by *all* the participants? Meetings embody the culture of an organization more than any other single activity. In a sense, meetings *are* the culture. Meetings shout out the company's true values.

> " The ultimate ownership of meetings is demonstrated when every participant takes responsibility to embody the core values of the organization. "

It begins with the way a meeting is structured, and it keeps appearing in how the meeting is managed. The culture will be on full display in presenting, discussion, decision-making, energy levels, and even in freedom for participants to express themselves.

Meetings need established ground rules that apply equally to everyone. These ground rules should expressly reinforce the stated values of the company and, more specifically, its meeting values. The ultimate ownership of meetings is demonstrated when every participant takes responsibility to embody the core values of the organization. Think of meeting ground rules as unique to your culture. In establishing them, don't look for someone else's list. Rather, start with an existing ground rule that is already well-embodied and build from there.

No one merely attends the meeting as a spectator. Everyone owns the productivity of the meeting and their role as a contributor. Participants must feel responsible to voice their concerns and share their opinions. This sense of ownership molds participants into a unified body, all in step with the action. Who owns the meeting? *Everyone.* Joy is the reward for owning the meeting together. "Complete my joy by being of the same mind, having the same love, being in full accord and of one mind" (Philippians 2:2).

> **" If you value a meeting skill, recognize and compliment people for demonstrating it. "**

Improve Meeting Skills

Ownership of anything should involve its care, growth, and improvement. When we own something of value, we preserve and care for it. Without a sense of ownership, we tend to use something as if we're only renting it. We subtly, if not openly, extract its value without the long-term view of investment and growth.

Meeting ownership includes improving. In this sense, all participants own the meeting and do their part to lift the meeting to the next level. The process of "leveling up" will be addressed in chapter 14.

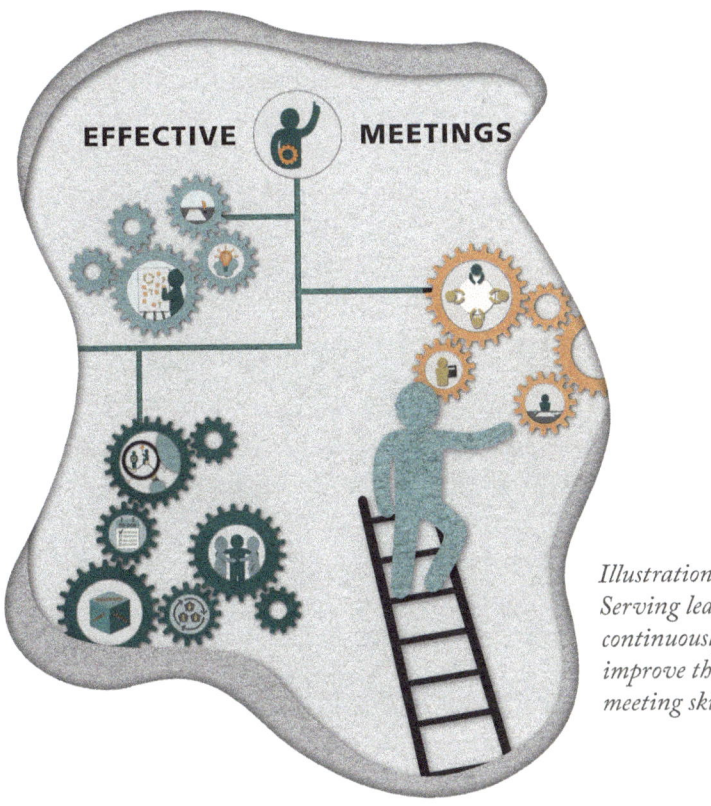

Illustration 11: Serving leaders continuously improve their meeting skills.

59

Here are questions to guide development of meeting skills:

- What vision do you have to improve meetings?
- Do you train or coach participants to show up owning their part?
- Do you coach your team on how to structure meetings, and to facilitate, prepare presentations, engage, and debate?
- Do you guide them on how to build momentum for increasing the synergy of the discussion and to contribute with positive energy?
- Have you considered scoring your meetings?
- Is meeting performance part of the job description and reflected in the job review?

One of the most practical ways to improve your meetings as a team is to identify the strengths and weaknesses of the group. *The Serving Leader Meeting Assessment* (see chapter 14) is a comprehensive evaluation representing meeting skills. Out of these skills, select five to improve on. Assess your meetings regularly, practicing and honing these five skills until desired improvement occurs. Then choose another five skills for the group to focus on (see illustration 11). To gain insight into the group's learning process, carve out the last couple minutes of each meeting to evaluate the five skills being worked on.

In practicing meeting skills, it's important not only to demonstrate the behaviors you wish others to imitate, but also to reward those behaviors. If you value a meeting skill, recognize and compliment people for demonstrating it. When a captivating presentation is given, praise the presenter. When great visuals are used to communicate, point this out. When someone asks great questions during a tough discussion, highlight their contribution. When someone objects and raises the flag of healthy debate, honor their bravery.

The apostle Paul said it best: "Be imitators of me, as I am of Christ" (1 Corinthians 11:1). By your example, build a meeting culture that requires participants to show up, fully participate, and own their part with an eye towards improving.

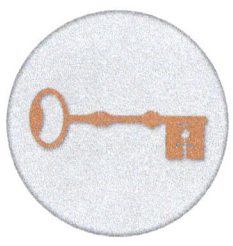

Here are key indicators of a lack of ownership:

- little felt sense of expectation for improving meetings
- core values missing from meeting culture
- little energy going into measuring or evaluating meeting skills
- no training or mentoring offered to improve meetings
- good meeting behaviors or skills going unacknowledged by the leader

Meeting Types

Ray made his strong recommendation to completely revamp AgSalt's meetings immediately after sitting in his first meeting. Unbeknownst to me, he politely asked to meet with me alone to save me from being embarrassed in front of my business partners. As they exited the meeting, Ray turned to me and asked, "Did this meeting represent a typical meeting for you?"

"Yes, it felt quite normal," I responded. "I'm curious. What did you think?"

Instead of answering, Ray responded, "How do you compare your meetings with what you saw in Elam's meetings at Country Value Woodworks?"

Illustration 12:
Serving leaders design a
unique set of meetings that
best serve their organization.

"Well," I said, "I suppose our meetings are as warm and congenial as Elam's." Ray paused a moment, then replied. "True. You're a very kind and empathetic leader. How else would you compare Elam's meetings with what you see in your own?" This time I paused. "To be honest, Elam's meetings are very different. That's why I hired you!"

Ray breathed a sigh of relief and smiled, "Then you want my thoughts on the matter?" I nodded. Ray continued, "Your meetings are quite lacking. There is plenty of graciousness in the room but not much structure, nor good facilitation—not to mention a lack of ownership."

Ray went on for a while, critiquing my way of doing meetings. When he finished, I wasn't feeling very good about myself. So many things were wrong with my meetings! Ray had an eagle's eye. I felt like his penetrating look saw nothing but blemishes, and there was no one but myself to blame. I lowered my head but then lifted it and looked Ray in the eye. "I've

got an honest question. How do I learn to love it when I'm the problem?"

Ray went on to cast a vision that included how he would coach me in leading better meetings. He described both a disciplined approach and how he would help me distinguish between meeting types.

Meeting types are a way of differentiating between meetings that differ in purpose, structure, and content. For example, the purpose of a brainstorming meeting is very different from getting together for the purpose of deciding which bid to choose for a building project. Once separated, different meeting types can be fit together to form a complete set or system of meetings (see illustration 12). This system is flexible, allowing several types of meetings to be combined into one meeting. For example, a smaller or younger organization can use a handful of core meetings with different types of meetings combined into one to meet their needs. One meeting in the system naturally leads to the next, creating an effective meeting sequence. A larger organization can choose to expand their meeting system to include many different types of meetings to more effectively guide all the moving parts.

As an organization grows in size, a set of various meeting types is increasingly needed. This section will clarify which meetings are foundational and fundamental for good communication and direction to flow from inside the head of the leader to the frontline workers and other stakeholders. They help to identify what you need or don't need for a fully equipped meeting toolbox, unique to your company's size and complexity. As J. Elise Keith says in *Where the Action Is,* "When you understand each type of meeting and how to use them together to accomplish your goals, it becomes possible to use meetings as tools for streamlining your business operations."[10]

Why is a system or structure of meeting types important? Why does it matter? What outcomes or benefits are realized?

Like the building contractor with an incomplete set of tools, a meeting leader is limited and crippled by missing tools. But with the right tools, management frustrations disappear and new possibilities are realized. However, like the expert craftsman with skillful hands on the tool, you must understand and hone each meeting's purpose and function to lead it effectively. Learning how to distinguish among different types of meetings, and how to use them as a set, is akin to the contractor pulling onto the job site fully equipped and skilled with tools. Just like a saw has a different function than a hammer, different types of meetings provide different functions.

> " **Imagine a system of meetings reducing your management load and creating momentum as your people gain clarity and hold each other accountable, leading to a life-giving work culture. "**

Simplicity comes by clearly understanding what types of meetings are needed for your size of organization. What meetings do you need? Where do you start?

Don't let the idea of many different types of meetings make your head spin. These meeting types are simply one system broken out into three categories. The point of listing and briefly describing these types is not to imply you need to use every type, but rather to give you a menu and quick glimpse of each, from which you can custom build the best system of meetings for your organization.

To extend the building contractor analogy, tools and expertise aren't nearly as beneficial without a set of blueprints to custom build the house. This meeting blueprint is equivalent to a system of meetings broken into three categories with individual types of meetings. Each type of meeting does not stand alone, but is connected to the whole.

Like blueprints, a set of meetings must be engineered and designed with a touch of architectural beauty for your unique organization. Using your tools to slap together a house without a blueprint is like running meetings with no system while hoping to create a beautiful, functioning organization.

Leading a beautifully designed set of meetings that flow together will benefit your organization in a myriad of ways. This way of doing things will give your organization life by eliminating the chaos that naturally arises when meeting systems aren't in place. Precious time being tied up with ineffective or inefficient meetings, random conversations here and there that pull you apart in multiple directions while you're trying to keep everything in your head—all this is eliminated. Imagine a system of meetings reducing your management load and creating momentum as your people gain clarity and hold each other accountable, leading to a life-giving work culture.

This section identifies types of meetings grouped into three categories:

Foundational Meetings

These meetings are rhythmic, occurring regularly, typically attended by the same people, and address the core needs of the organization. For example, they are planned throughout the year to ensure annual planning gets broken down into quarterly goals that are then worked out into weekly and daily tasks.

Building-block Meetings

These meetings are singularly focused to explore issues of any size with adequate time allocated and the right people handpicked for the purpose of the meeting.

Relational Meetings

These meetings are characterized by people coming together to enjoy each other, share information, resolve conflict, and learn new skills and procedures. Such meetings are particularly culture shaping and are designed to build relationships, trust, and identity.

Chapter Eight

Foundational Meetings

To make meetings more effective, we need to have multiple types of meetings, and clearly distinguish between the various purposes, formats, and timing of those meetings.

PATRICK LENCIONI, *Death by Meeting*

Foundational meetings are the central hub from which people drive work momentum and accomplish the mission—linchpin meetings. Like a beating heart, the rhythm becomes more intense if the organizational load is heavy. A consistent rhythmic heartbeat is a trademark of foundational meetings.

In the early days at AgSalt, there was no rhythm to our meetings. We had an irregular heartbeat. Issues, chaos, and troubles piled up until someone voiced enough frustration to force a meeting.

Serving leaders should gather their people regularly to meet, discuss, and decide about the recurring issues of organizational life. The hallmark of this set of meetings is they happen at regular, predictable intervals with typically the same people involved. Their structure and process support the mission, strategic objectives, and operational aspects of the business. Foundational meetings start with big-picture annual meetings

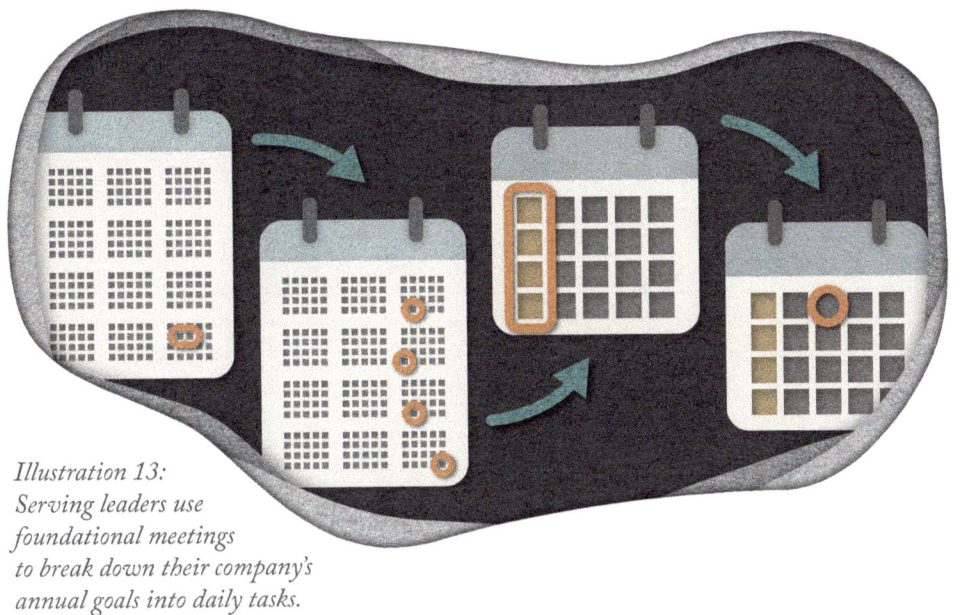

*Illustration 13:
Serving leaders use
foundational meetings
to break down their company's
annual goals into daily tasks.*

and cascade down to quarterly meetings, then on to weekly and daily meetings (see illustration 13).

But these meetings can morph into boring and ineffective routines. Same people, same room, same agenda format, same old plodding along in a rut of not-so-great meetings. The serving leader must rise to the challenge of designing and building their foundational meetings into life-giving discussions.

This is done by infusing foundational meetings with effective disciplines: structure, facilitation, engagement, synergy, and ownership. As J. Elise Keith says in *Where the Action Is,*

> *These are the meetings where your team sees you live your values (or not), where great ideas get shared (or not), where you learn about tricky problems on the horizon (or not), and where your team members renew their commitment to each other and your organization's mission (or not).*[11]

If your organization is small (fewer than 25 people), you will likely only need to use the foundational meetings listed below and a few of the relational meetings (see chapter 10). If you're new to the idea of different types, start by building out this foundational set.

The set of six foundational meetings include:

1. annual strategic planning meetings
2. quarterly leadership meetings
3. weekly management meetings
4. daily check-in meetings
5. one-on-one meetings
6. board governance or owner meetings

Because foundational meetings are so important, I designed step-by-step guides for several foundational meeting types, including weekly management and direct-report one-on-one meetings (see section five). These guides are detailed and provide a practical, actionable path to integrating the 3D approach (meeting disciplines, types, and levels) into these crucial meetings.

For larger organizations, building-block and relational meetings function as spillover meetings because the topics tend to be larger and take more time than a foundational meeting can allow. Like a lake held behind a dam, foundational meetings can hold only so much water. Large issues can hijack the conversation if you don't have a spillover reservoir built into your meeting design. Even smaller organizations have knotty issues that cannot be handled in the sixty to ninety minutes of a weekly management meeting. As soon as it's evident the issue is too big for a foundational meeting, move it to a building-block or relational meeting.

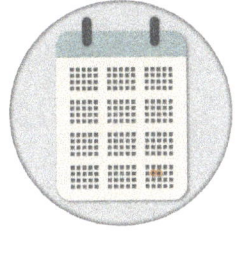

Annual Strategic Planning Meeting

The annual strategic planning meeting is known by many names throughout the business community: annual planning, strategic planning, and long-term vision casting. Whatever it's called, this meeting is inherently forward-looking. While the focus is on strategic objectives for the upcoming year and reflecting on the shortcomings of the previous year, the annual strategic planning meeting also projects vision for the next three, five, or ten years. This meeting produces an annual plan that considers the business model, market, core values, strategies, and resources of the organization.

The businesses I interviewed for this guide all have incorporated some version of this planning event. An effective annual strategic planning meeting is the difference between a business that's on a trajectory toward a destination and one that's going somewhere, but no one knows where.

Country Value, for instance, has always been a forward-looking organization because Elam is a visionary leader. However, his creative horsepower was trapped inside because he didn't have a framework in place for creating and sharing his strategic vision with his people.

When Ray explained this to Elam, it sparked Country Value's first annual strategic planning meeting. Elam brought his visionary power and enlisted input from the entire team, and together they mapped out the company's future for the next three to five years. At the same time, they planned how the people within the business would carry out that vision.

> **"** A serving leader gives people at all levels of the organization the opportunity to speak into emerging plans. **"**

Annual strategic planning meetings occur once a year and may require two or three days of work. The preparation for these meetings is significant. Some organizations spread these days of meetings across a month. A serving leader gives people at all levels of the organization the opportunity to speak into emerging plans. At Toyota, leadership engages the entire hierarchy to some degree in the conversation about the company's plans. This openness connects employees to the company's mission and creates feelings of belonging and being valued. What results is a "business plan with a heartbeat," a saying coined by David Bower of Seven Oaks Landscaping.

Quarterly Leadership Meeting

The quarterly leadership meeting is a short-term planning meeting focused on solving issues and setting goals. The purpose of the quarterly leadership meeting is to assess the progress made toward reaching the annual goals, and to reset quarterly plans to align with strategies, wins, challenges, or new information. It creates space for the team to reflect and discuss the state of the organization and to strengthen team synergy.

Who belongs at the table for these quarterly meetings? Pioneer Equipment's president, Daniel Wengerd, says their quarterly meetings involve not just the department heads, but also people who've served with the company long enough to care about its direction and have insight for the future. At Pioneer's quarterly meetings, updates are provided on the direction of the business, and half the meeting time is providing information. Daniel said, "We give out financial reports and review the budget. We spend the rest of the time getting feedback… It has been very positive in pulling the team together. We've got some tremendous talent at the table."

> " Large issues can crop up and threaten the momentum achieved in these weekly meetings, so be quick to schedule a building-block or relational meeting to give more attention and time to the problem. "

Depending on the size of organization, quarterly leadership meetings take up to a full day. This meeting reviews the last ninety days, realigning with the organization's annual goals and core values. It then solves higher-level issues plaguing the company and sets goals for the next quarter. This includes reaching a consensus on who's doing what, allocating the resources to accomplish it.

Weekly Management Meeting

The weekly management meeting is tactical—a hands-on approach to steering the machine of weekly operations and day-to-day issues. It's not a planning meeting or a meeting to re-strategize and think big picture, but rather to squarely face the immediate problems and challenges of the current week. This meeting is typically sixty to ninety minutes long, and all managers should be present.

This meeting opens with connecting as a team, then moves on to sharing important information, reviewing metrics, and resolving issues. Each attendee reports on the status of their to-dos from the previous week, but most of the meeting is spent discussing relevant topics. Large issues can crop up and threaten the momentum achieved in these meetings, so be quick to schedule a building-block or relational meeting to give more attention and time to the problem.

Note: A step-by-step Serving Leader guide is dedicated to the correct execution of this meeting: *The Weekly Management Meeting Guide*. While the guide focuses on managers and executives, the weekly management meeting can be adapted to fit any level of weekly meeting throughout an organization.

Daily Check-In Meeting

The daily check-in meeting has many labels—the daily huddle, the hand-off meeting, the daily stand-up meeting, the kickoff meeting, and other such names. It has various applications such as a shift hand-off between managers, or starting off with reflection from yesterday and a quick rundown of the day ahead.

The purpose of this meeting, according to Patrick Lencioni, "is to help team members avoid confusion about how priorities are translated into action on a regular basis. It provides a quick forum for ensuring nothing falls through the cracks on a given day and no one steps on anyone else's toes."[12] Daily check-ins also handle issues that pop up throughout the day. The meetings are run quickly and efficiently, averaging between five to fifteen minutes.

Before I understood how types of meetings work together, I leaned too heavily on the daily meeting. They became time consuming and a

> " **Many issues that come up in organizations can be worked out with the efficiency of one-on-one meetings, rather than consuming valuable group time.** "

disruption to my work, filling my day with constant interruptions. While daily check-ins have their place, be careful not to overuse it or replace the weekly management meeting with these conversations. However, when used in conjunction with a complete set of foundational meetings, the daily meeting is an indispensable little tool.

One-on-One Meeting

One-on-one meetings are used to build relationships, offer encouragement, and develop accountability and trust between two parties. Many issues that come up in organizations can be worked out with the efficiency of one-on-one meetings, rather than consuming valuable group time.

The most common one-on-one meeting is between a manager and an employee, but other examples include coaching or mentoring, client check-ins, and meetings between colleagues. These one-on-one conversations provide a place for work or personal discussions that help foster individual growth.

Everyone needs that personal touch of meaningful conversation about things that matter to them. For example, a client may need a personal call to clear up questions or be assured of the project timeline. In the case of a direct report and manager, these one-on-one meetings need to be scheduled regularly. This connection time should be structured so the conversation is casual and warm.

Note: A step-by-step Serving Leader guide is dedicated to the correct execution of a one-on-one meeting between a manager and their direct report: *The Direct Report One-on-One Meeting Guide.*

Board Governance or Owner Meeting

At board governance or owner meetings, business owners, board members, or other stakeholders gather to discuss governance matters such as organizational strategy, ownership items, or other high-level planning.

These meetings need regular attention and rhythm. They take place monthly, quarterly, or—at a minimum—annually, sometimes being bound by legalities and official meeting records.

Owner or shareholder meetings typically address issues like family members' participation in the business, leadership transition processes, financial ownership percentages, review of buy/sell agreements, annual distribution of dividends, and other governance issues.

For nonprofit organizations, the board members aren't usually involved in daily administration, so their governance function must be reinforced with a well-run board meeting guided by clear policies and procedures. These meetings often include time spent with the administrative team to review operational reports and to make high-level operational decisions.

Planning is essential for all meetings, but especially for this one. The tone is set by sending a complete and detailed agenda out days in advance with assigned meeting roles. Sometimes having conversations with participants about major topics before the meeting can be helpful. This type of meeting is like the rudder of a ship where the best minds join together to steer the organization and create the future together.

Chapter Nine
Building-Block Meetings

*No meeting works on its own. The outcomes from one meeting are
used to start the discussion in another meeting.*

J. ELISE KEITH, *Where the Action Is*

Building-block meetings provide singleness of focus and adequate
time to explore any size issue with the right people around the table.

Building-block meetings are either a single meeting in your meeting
system or an element of a meeting. Here are four ways building-block
meetings can be used:

1. as a single-topic meeting
2. as an extension from another meeting where an issue
   needed more time
3. as a staple element, in part, of another type of meeting, and not
   as an entirely separate meeting type
4. as a workshop, combining individual building-block meetings into one

When held as a single-topic meeting, building-block meetings can be
singularly focused on one item or issue. Being singularly focused allows
for agendas that drill down into an array of details and nuances. As
such, leaders can use a single-focused meeting completely customized
with the right mix of people concentrating on one thing. For example, a
brainstorming meeting could be focused on a new product or reinvent a
problematic process in order to yield higher returns.

When held as an extension from another meeting, building-block
meetings are scheduled as needed, often triggered by issues or situations
that need more time than other meetings can provide. These issues may
need hours to find answers, not minutes. In this sense, building-block
meetings provide a spillover function for larger issues that don't fit, as
well as for items that clearly need a separate meeting to address topics
more thoroughly.

When incorporated as a staple element in another type of meeting,
building-block meetings are used in part, and not as a whole, and
integrated into another meeting's agenda. For example, in a foundational meeting, you could integrate elements of a problem-solving,
brainstorming, planning, or decision-making meeting. For smaller
organizations, integrating staple elements of building-block meetings

into foundational meetings is often the go-to method, thus making it unnecessary to schedule separate building-block meetings.

When combined as individual building-block meetings, these meeting types create a workshop. This integrates these individual meetings into a whole, not just elements—a single longer meeting. For example, a workshop may start with a brainstorming meeting. Once the brainstorming meeting concludes, it's followed by a planning meeting, using the idea discovered in the brainstorming process. Once a plan is proposed using the planning meeting process, a decision-making meeting is held to finalize the idea. These multiple types of meetings are woven together seamlessly back-to-back, to effectively accomplish the purpose of the workshop.

Illustration 14: Serving leaders use building-block meetings to serve the needs of a company that extend beyond the rhythm of foundational meetings.

The set of eight building-block meetings include:

1. problem-solving meetings
2. understanding meetings
3. brainstorming meetings
4. planning meetings
5. decision-making meetings
6. progress meetings
7. action reviews
8. workshops (see illustration 14)

Problem-Solving Meeting

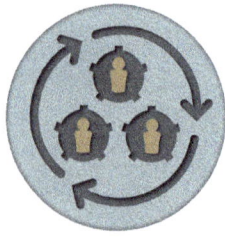

No business operates and grows without its fair share of challenges. Problem-solving meetings are where teams analyze, deliberate, and hash out tough issues to find a workable solution and implement an action plan. It may involve an operational issue, major project challenge, or an incident response.

Most, but not all, problem-solving activity is best done in a small meeting at the location of the problem, not in some executive meeting room. Problem-solving must include gathering data, research, and experimentation on-site and within the working environment. Once a hypothesis, root cause, or countermeasure is determined, experiments must be done to either confirm or refute it. Only after this on-site work is performed can a group discussion away from the site of the problem be effective. As such, many problems never need a group meeting. Going too quickly to group discussion discounts the influence of human flaws such as bias, assumptions, jumping to conclusions, and lack of pattern recognition. When a group problem-solving meeting is convened, of course the goal is to solve the problem, but the temptation to fill knowledge gaps and jump to uninformed solutions is nearly irresistible and occurs naturally without any warning that it has happened. However, without support of facts, group problem-solving meetings are an illusion.

At Seven Oaks, when faced with a repetitive problem, they sent two people to where leaf removal teams were working and observed them. After a while, they stopped the crews and asked simple questions like, "What do you think is going well?" and "What would you do differently?" This valuable intel brought back to the conference room brought the insight they needed to solve the problem, and a new company standard of removing leaves was set.

> " **Going too quickly to group discussion discounts the influence of human flaws such as bias, assumptions, jumping to conclusions, and lack of pattern recognition.** "

Problem-solving meetings typically take thirty to ninety minutes, depending on the complexity of the problem. The meeting should begin with defining and understanding the problem and analyzing it by asking, "What's the problem?" as determined from the people closest to it. Then explore "Why does the problem exist?" Solution goals and constraints around the discussion will help the team move toward a workable solution. The team then brainstorms and discusses possible outcomes, weighing pros and cons. Once there's agreement, an action plan is created with accountability and follow-up to ensure success.

Understanding Meeting

Sometimes you need to get together to make sense of something. The purpose of an understanding meeting is to learn as a group and gain insight on a topic or situation. This could take the form of consulting with your team members on a matter of research, clarifying a standard operating procedure, or meeting to get on the same page. This type of meeting could also be used to find out what really happened and who's responsible, as would be the case in investigating a work accident.

Understandings are often woven as an element throughout the weekly management meeting, and are included in meeting notes for clarity.

Prepare by collecting the information you have on the subject, including anything you can hunt down yourself, and jot down questions you need answers to. During the meeting, lay out the information along with your questions, and then allow the group to talk without interruption. Use your listening posture to find answers to the questions brought to the group.

This meeting isn't designed for the group to talk through or hash out an issue—that's a problem-solving meeting. An understanding meeting is structured to limit participants to seek insight from each other. A few clarifying questions can be useful to deepen understanding. Wrap up the meeting by sharing insights gained from the discussion, then choose the next steps

Brainstorming Meeting

A brainstorming meeting is designed to serve a group of people who need to creatively generate new ideas. Begin by organizing the discussion around a clear purpose. Define the constraints that apply to the project, and specify how the ideas will be used afterward. Some people may bring their best ideas if given the purpose, restraints, and intended use ahead of time with space to brainstorm before the meeting.

These discussions could look like drafting a list of potential new products, planning an ad campaign, or creating ways to engage people in the company culture. Brainstorming meetings can also kick off a workshop followed by other combined types of meetings.

Write down all ideas. Even those that seem out in left field can inspire creativity that could lead to a workable idea. No idea is a dumb idea, so eliminate commenting on the merit of all ideas during this stage.

Wrap up the meeting by reviewing what was produced. Depending on the goals, the group may need to choose the top ideas and determine next steps. Finally, determine how those ideas will be applied or implemented.

Pioneer IWS, a minimalist industrial shelving solution that could be assembled without tools or screws, was still just an idea when Doug Sheetz came on as the marketing director at Pioneer Equipment.

Doug remembered how the brothers leading the business approached him about the project. "They said, 'Well, we have this thing.' And they showed me what they had, this one rack in a back corner. 'We really think this is marketable, but we're not there yet,' they told me."

The "thing" the Wengerd brothers described was something that had been dreamed up with the robotic welder one day. It was a LEGO® system on steroids, and Pioneer needed to know if it had a leg to stand on.

Doug continued, "We set up a weekly meeting with Larry and John from research and development, and Daniel as needed. We started looking at this 'thing.' What is it? What do we have? What makes it unique?" This was a brainstorming meeting at its finest.

Planning Meeting

Planning meetings bring a team together to form a plan and secure commitment to making it happen. This could take the form of project planning, event planning, or designing a marketing plan. These meetings typically range from thirty minutes to three hours, and may be used as an element of another type of meeting. A planning meeting generally doesn't start with a blank slate, but with a rough framework already in place.

When the meeting starts, cover the goal, the process to get there, and an idea of what the results could look like. Then fill in the details of the plan, review it, and confirm next steps, including how you'll communicate progress on the plan.

Note: The annual strategic planning meeting (foundational meeting) is a stand-alone meeting type because it combines elements of different types of meetings and is not just a planning meeting.

Decision-Making Meeting

Making decisions is a critical part of organizational life. A decision-making meeting brings together the right group of people to decide between two or more choices. Decisions such as hiring or firing, final approvals, or a yes or no choice are all examples of what can happen during a decision-making meeting.

Preparation before a decision is critical, because if research is incomplete or information is missing or attendees aren't given enough time to process the information, the meeting can have poor results. More time will be needed if choosing from more than two options.

If a decision-making process isn't already established, be sure to select one. Common processes include majority vote, unanimous consensus, or one person deciding after seeking input. In *Bad Meetings Happen to Good People*, Leigh Espy writes, "When meeting participants are involved in the decision-making process, they feel more buy-in and ownership of the decision that's been made."[13]

Present the information, then debate and discuss the options. Consensus can be built during this stage by people hearing each other's pros and cons. Next, use your decision-making process to decide. Secure commitments and decide on next steps, which may include making an announcement or a planning meeting to carry the decision forward. Don't forget to document these important decisions.

Progress Meeting

A progress meeting helps maintain your organization's momentum on a particular project that needs guidance. For leadership teams, this naturally happens inside the weekly management meeting, but progress meetings can be used company-wide to provide accountability and support for the projects or performance that needs monitoring.

For example, a manager who isn't involved in senior leadership can use a progress meeting to check in with a crew's project. Progress meetings can be internal, such as a project status meeting, or external, like a client update meeting. These meetups can be anywhere from fifteen minutes to an hour, depending how often they're scheduled or the size of the project.

In *Where the Action Is*, J. Elise Keith describes these kinds of meeting as "lean, mean performance machines."[14]

For internal meetings, identify tasks or roadblocks needing attention, share information, and make any needed course corrections. For external meetings, the focus is often on updating the client, answering questions, and building the relationship

Action Review

The purpose of an action review is to learn from past successes and failures and confidently move forward on how to improve. These types of meetings can be held after a project completion, after a sales win or loss, after an annual job review, or anywhere in your business where you want to improve your performance—even meetings!

At Country Value, an action review is held each day with the team leaders. They're asked, "How did yesterday go? What are the numbers telling us? What was the highest incident of rework? Did you confirm standard work?" Problems are addressed, problems are solved, and the work gets done.

Country Value is adept at measuring performance. They estimate and track productivity per man hour, which helps them set reasonable daily goals. A board over the production floor shows the team's progress toward their numbers. A clock displays how much time they have to reach this objective. This kind of data makes for effective action reviews because it helps to quantify progress.

The format of action review meetings is straightforward. Begin by reviewing the plan and facts about how it went. Then the group discusses what they learned.

Great questions are crucial in this process. The group then discusses and decides what they'll change in the future. These plans can always be experimental and adjusted as the team continues to learn.

The more often the team holds an action review, the faster the team will learn and improve together.

The meeting concludes with documenting any decisions or next steps.

Workshop

A workshop combines a variety of building-block meetings. A workshop typically includes these individual meetings as a whole, not just elements. As different meeting types are woven together, it creates focus and perspective that produces tangible results you wouldn't gain without this blending of meeting types.

The goal of each workshop is unique. For example, a workshop could be used to kick off a new project. Starting with a brainstorming meeting, this workshop would then head into developing a plan with a planning meeting, then adding in other types of meetings to accomplish the new initiative. A workshop could also be used to redesign the company web-site or to create synergy within a department via team-building exercises.

Because these types of meetings can cover several hours to days, pre-paring for one may take longer than the average meeting type. It may be worth the investment to bring in a facilitator or coach to increase productivity.

A workshop should be held in the normal workspace, and could open with a core values speech from a manager, a group icebreaker, or an overview of what's ahead.

The meat of the workshop will include the exercises or activities tar-geting the workshop goals. Refreshments and breaks boost morale and keep brains sharp. Wrap up by summarizing insights and knowledge gained, and by reviewing what was accomplished. Follow-up after the meeting will answer the question, "How will you use what you gained from the workshop?"

The annual workshop at Seven Oaks Landscaping is an all-day event looking back as well as forward. New goals are set, and accomplished goals are celebrated. The day is designed to be challenging but also fun, motivational, and rejuvenating. On the big day, the owners deliver a state-of-the-company overview, including statistics from the previous year, glows and grows (areas that were successful and areas that need improvement), and expectations for the coming year.

This is followed by breakout sessions where small groups discuss goals and how they'll meet them. This is an opportunity for employees to participate in shaping the company. For example, they can weigh in on how company funds should be allocated or what new equipment should be purchased.

They're also given projects to solve. One year, each group was required to develop a contingency plan in the event of work slowing down, and the group concluded they would prefer an across-the-board reduction in work hours instead of laying anyone off. A new policy was put in place as a result in case the situation were ever to occur.

This annual company-wide workshop reestablishes the company's commitment to give the employees the opportunity to shape company policy and culture. Every time it's held, it strengthens Seven Oaks' conviction that the company is all about people first, not numbers.

Chapter Ten
Relational Meetings

*People just like to be where people are enjoying themselves,
even—or should we say, especially—at work.*

JAMES KOUZES AND BARRY POSNER,
Encouraging the Heart

Relational meetings are uniquely life-giving because they give expression to relational values and foster connection with people. Life and work are about relationships. While all meetings should carry the cultural DNA of the company, it's this set of relational meetings that focus primarily on people meeting each other, knowing information, training together, socializing for fun, and—last but not least—healing broken and hurt relationships.

Relational meetings include the key culture-shaping events such as early morning meetings over coffee, fruit, and pastries. They include the summer company picnic, the Christmas banquet, and the birthday lunches. It's also meeting new people and feeling

> 66 **Building and restoring strong relationships at work is high on the list of priorities for the serving leader.** 99

Illustration 15: Serving leaders use relational meetings as key gatherings that shape the culture of the company.

the connection with customers and vendors at the customer appreciation days and industry shows or events. Relational meetings empower people and offer development with informational meetings and training in new skills (see illustration 15).

One of the most important relational meetings is redemptive and restorative. Even the most mature people offend and sin against others. In the serving leader's toolbox of meetings is the healing tool of mediation. These meetings are meant to work through the tough relational issues. Building and restoring strong relationships at work is high on the list of priorities for the serving leader.

Relational meetings include a set of five meeting types geared for building and maintaining relationships and empowering people with information and knowledge. The set of five relational meetings include:

1. introductions
2. announcement meetings
3. mediation meetings
4. trainings
5. culture meetings

Introductions

Meeting new people and forming new business connections is essential for relational health and well-being, especially for those who value community and relationships. Introductions help in discovering whether the parties should establish a new relationship or work together. Types of introductions may include job interviews; meeting other professionals, customers, or vendors for the first time; meet and greets; or prospective sales calls. These types of meetings can lead to new business relationships and ultimately lead to more understanding of the people in your world as you learn more about them. First impressions are key, so be prepared with confidence and knowledge of cultural etiquette.

> " Nothing ignites new relationship like genuine gratitude for being known and enjoyed. "

Doug from Pioneer Equipment recalls a time when they were pitching their product to Paul B. Zimmerman for the first time. He offered to go out to his car to grab another sample. When Doug got back, he was astounded to hear his coworker, the engineer, describing the product's flaws. Doug quickly changed the subject because it wasn't ready for market yet and he didn't want to leave a bad impression. When they finished pitching the product and got back to the car, Doug laughed and said, "I can't leave you alone for five minutes!"

Make sure you have a well-rehearsed authentic voice that communicates your values. In all introductions, be prepared to listen well and ask questions to uncover the information and feelings that spark relationship. At the end of an introduction meeting, state specific things you appreciated about the other person. Nothing ignites new relationship like genuine gratitude for being known and enjoyed.

Announcement Meeting

This type of meeting is used to share information with people either inside or outside the company. An internal announcement meeting could be a simple team update about a new hire or an all-hands-on-deck meeting during a crisis. External announcements can range from a new product launch or a statement on an important issue to the community.

No matter what announcement you're making, be honest and authentic, and give people the information they need to feel part of the team. Err on the side of over-communication versus under-communication because informing people is a way to honor them and fulfill your calling to shepherd them.

Knowing an announcement is coming can make people uncomfortable, even if the news is good. Understand this, and as a serving leader, craft a message that considers the perspective of the listener, remembering what people hear is more important than what you say (or thought you said). Your message should be designed to help get everyone on the same page, stay ahead of rumors, and allay fears. When dealing with a sensitive situation, consider informing select people in advance of the public announcement.

> " Err on the side of over-communication versus under-communication because informing people is a way to honor them and fulfill your calling to shepherd them. "

Begin by introducing your speakers. These persons should present the information as clearly as possible. Making time for questions or some other type of follow-up helps clear the air and correct false assumptions about the announcement. Following up can sometimes be done through an email or another meeting breaking down a situation in practical terms for each team member.

Mediation Meeting

Unfortunately, at times two parties firmly disagree on how a particular problem should be solved. Relationships can be injured or broken, thus needing a mediation meeting to try and work things out. Personal or team conflicts, partner disagreements, contract negotiations and disputes, and other situations may require a mediation meeting to find a way forward toward compromise, healing, and restored respect. These meetings test even the most experienced leader and call for emotional intelligence and wisdom to walk the path of mediation. Ideally, an agreement or resolution between parties is the end goal, with clarity around how to move forward or rebuild trust. This may involve a new agreement, deeper commitment to relationship, or reconciliation.

Resolving issues arising from personal disagreements, differing values, and misconduct are especially painful, and closure doesn't always feel good to everyone involved. The meeting must not be dictated by emotions; rather, emotions need to be managed and acknowledged, honoring the cry of pain. This creates a path toward vulnerability with appropriate boundaries. To increase the chance of a positive outcome, it's often helpful to involve a mediator or neutral party.

> " **Articulating what could happen if the meeting fails can motivate participants to find a workable solution.** "

After Saul's conversion on the road to Damascus and his return to Jerusalem, "he attempted to join the disciples. And they were all afraid of him, for they did not believe that he was a disciple" (Acts 9:26). Barnabas called a mediation meeting and "brought him to the apostles and declared to them how on the road he had seen the Lord, who spoke to him, and how at Damascus he had preached boldly in the name of Jesus" (Acts 9:27). In this role, Barnabas bridged the gap between the previous persecutor and his new Christian family.

Articulating what could happen if the meeting fails can motivate participants to find a workable solution. Begin the meeting by highlighting humility, mercy, or your commitment to enter conflict and to suffer with the situation. Establish where you already have agreement, then actively listen to both sides without interruption. Ask clarifying questions to erase misunderstanding. Once the situation is thoroughly understood, work through the conflict to find a compromise both parties can live with. Don't forget to follow up when needed to ensure the negotiation was a success.

Training

While training must be a part of any organization, it's ineffective whenever the atmosphere of learning isn't valued. Clear examples of training inside a company are onboarding new employees, educating customers, running safety trainings, and much more.

For effective training meetings, develop clear objectives and enlist qualified personnel as teachers. A key to the success of this type of meeting for the trainee to bring a commitment to learn along with attentiveness and willingness to engage.

Company training often has the reputation for being boring, producing disengaged attendees who are there only because their boss required it. Listening to feedback from your participants provides ideas for improving the training next time.

This type of meeting can also be a tool for leaders who want to bring people up through the ranks. Training is critical in any organization that cares about developing leaders and enabling employees' growth. Training is the door to new knowledge and skills, which in turn will expand an organization's confidence and competence.

Culture Meeting

Culture meetings create a sense of belonging for those who choose to participate, since mandatory attendance isn't usually required. Most of these meetings create space for people to share life, exchange ideas, and develop connections around festivity and celebrations.

Examples of this type of meeting include company picnics, banquets, and birthdays, meeting up with other like-minded employees or business owners, or lunch and learns. Planning is needed, but no agenda is required to make these meetings succeed. The heartbeat of the culture is often maintained and nurtured with these relationally rich times of connection.

One of the most essential meetings held at Seven Oaks is their morning culture meeting. This meeting happens at 6:45 a.m. when the foremen and leaders show up for their daily check-in meeting. During this time, they ensure all logistics about the day are understood. However, the entire company is welcome to come before their shift at 7:00 a.m. Coffee is served, and most if not all of the employees show up, though they're not required to be there. The space Seven Oaks creates for these employees to socialize with other team members builds relationships and strengthens their culture.

> " Training is the door to new knowledge and skills, which in turn will expand an organization's confidence and competence. "

When COVID struck in 2020 and the company could no longer hold this culture meeting in the mornings, in the words of their president David Bower, "It just about destroyed us."

When the maintenance department employees at Seven Oaks were asked what this culture meeting meant to them, one person responded, "When we're there, we're all on the same ground. We're all at the same level." David remarked that the laborers love the informal interaction they get with management during this meeting. What naturally happens is shop talk integrates with family and personal conversations. Foremen are as likely to be showing photos of their new baby as they are to be showing photos of the day's project. It's a time to connect, build camaraderie, and get everyone ready for the day.

Meeting Levels

I still remember the day a brand-new John Deere 4020 tractor was delivered to our farm on the back of a rollback truck. I was six years old, and that tractor looked huge to me!

My dad was always a John Deere man, and though we already had a 2020 (50 horsepower) and a 2520 (60 horsepower) on the farm, this was truly something else. At 100 horsepower, the new 4020 could pull a five-bottom plow or a fourteen-foot disk, something those other tractors just couldn't do. It was a major improvement for Dad's growing operation.

Like tractors, meetings have a horsepower rating that power the progress and efficiency of an organization (see illustration 16). Basic meetings, like the 50 horsepower tractor, do well with small loads, and intermediate meetings can pull the weight of a larger organization or issue. But it's advanced meetings that can handle the heaviest and most critical loads.

Just as my dad knew he needed a more powerful tractor for his farm, a growing organization must learn to hold meetings that can deal with the strain the business bears. Like most larger farms, there's still a place for the smaller tractors. Likewise, larger companies may still have some use for smaller horse-powered meetings.

Illustration 16: A serving leader uses the right level for their organizational load.

The three levels of meetings represent a simple model you can use to identify what level of meetings you currently have, and to evaluate your meeting capacity and power. Leading your meetings to the next level requires honing your skills in each of the meeting disciplines. Turning up the horsepower requires increasing the intensity of these disciplines—more structure, better facilitation, greater engagement, closer synergy, and increasing ownership when leveling up.

These three levels of meetings are not rigid categories. It's not uncommon for an organization to function primarily within a certain level, but to also use a mix of meeting skills from the next level up or down. Adding new meeting skills—or simply improving a skill—is the way to move to the next level.

A serving leader matches the level of horsepower needed for the organization's size, complexity, and strain. Using the right meeting level for your situation is common sense like a farmer choosing the right size tractor to get the job done.

What's important is to identify which level of meeting is right for you, then design your meeting structure and scale your skills accordingly.

One of the common themes of fast-growing companies is that strong sales opportunities tend to force human energy and resources to serve the customer. As a result, company structure, including meetings, doesn't often develop enough to handle the strain, causing frustration and chaos. AgSalt was a classic case. In the first twenty years, I never viewed meetings as the hub of the organization. From the concept of levels and horsepower, AgSalt used a very basic level of meetings or a small tractor. This worked until we started growing over 30% per year for several consecutive years. When we finally hired Ray to help, our meetings could have been compared to using a 50 horsepower tractor to pull a 100 horsepower load. We were using basic-level meetings but badly needed advanced-level meetings. This is why Ray suggested a complete overhaul of our meetings, not just a tune up. For AgSalt, this meant learning a host of new meeting disciplines and skills over a period of one year. This short time frame was needed because we had to quickly move up approximately a whole meeting level.

This section identifies three levels of meeting:

 **Basic Meetings**

 **Intermediate Meetings**

 **Advanced Meetings**

BASIC

Chapter Eleven
Basic Meetings

On the farm where I grew up, I received my own introduction to basic meetings—though I didn't call it that back then.

My brother Laverne and I joined the farm partnership with my dad in our late teen years. We rarely sat down to have a formal meeting. Instead, most meetings were held as we leaned on the cattle gate or while milking the cows. We never used terms like agenda, discussion points, or tabled items. And meeting minutes were simply stored in our heads. When things needed discussion, we would simply pause and hash out the issue, then keep moving forward.

Life on the farm was simple and needed only basic-level discussions to maintain a shared perspective. In our little world, that was generally adequate, but operating without a formal meeting structure had its drawbacks. We had our share of misunderstandings and lack of communication. I had a long way to go before I would cut my teeth as a serving leader. I had yet to learn about discerning which meeting level was best for the job and which skills were required to lead it.

> **" At the basic level, meeting structure is largely shaped and run by one individual—the person in charge. "**

Basic meetings happen when groups of people get together to discuss, plan, or make a decision without being guided by a well-defined meeting structure—the first discipline. Basic meetings tend to be the least formal of all servant-led meetings, but that doesn't make them bad. Instead, basic meetings are often held as needed (without being scheduled ahead of time) or handled as on-the-go discussions. Typically, very few standard processes or procedures govern them.

An informal stand-up meeting in the maintenance shop is a good example of a basic meeting. So is the one-on-one meeting held at an employee's workbench. In that sense, these events may bear little resemblance to the formal sit-down gatherings we usually associate with the word "meeting."

If run well, basic meetings can be sufficient for smaller organizations or start-ups, for less formal occasions, or for lower-level department meetings within a larger organization. When it's just you and your boys running the farm or company—as my dad and his sons did for many years—you probably don't need a secretary, detailed minutes, or regularly scheduled meetings. But don't get me wrong—any of these could be helpful and worth exploring to increase meeting efficiency in any size organization.

Basic meetings may or may not include a written agenda. Formal ground rules are minimal. As J. Elise Keith notes in *Where the Action Is,*

> *When a company is small, it's pretty easy to maintain a shared perspective, and it's okay to simply schedule a meeting whenever you need one. You're busy, and you have a good idea of what everyone else is doing each day, so you really need to meet only when you get stuck.*[15]

At the basic level, meeting structure (preparing, leading, following up) is largely shaped and run by one individual—the person in charge. In fact, the person leading a basic meeting likely learned how to do so on their own or from having watched someone else do it.

It's up to the serving leader to ensure meetings run with enough horsepower as it relates to the other disciplines of meeting facilitation, engagement, synergy, and ownership. If everyone knows each other well and individuals feel confident sharing their point of view, then basic meetings can work well with the simple application of the other disciplines.

One example where a basic meeting serves the needs of a larger organization is the daily check-in held at Seven Oaks Landscaping. At 6:45 a.m. each morning, the crew foremen and operations managers show up to get on the same page about the coming day. There's no "coming to order" as a group or set agenda. Discussion about the details of what needs to happen that day will take place over steaming cups of coffee and is frequently interrupted by swapping stories about their personal lives or greeting other arriving employees.

Basic meetings have their place in organizations of all shapes and sizes, but they're usually inadequate to address tasks that are more sizable and challenging. They often create chaos and frustration for organizations pulling heavier loads.

Another challenge of basic meetings is they rely on the leader who sets the meeting culture, whether they are competent in meeting skills or not.

Also, these unstructured times don't carry methods of accountability found in higher-level meetings. Meeting principles and practices are not in place to guard against lack of focus, distractions, and miscommunications.

Very small businesses using the basics can be surprisingly efficient and operate without conducting many formal meetings. And sometimes, this is sufficient for strong communication among members of the organization. In such a company, knowledge, strategy, and decisions are often managed on the go instead of directly in meetings. But be careful.

Nothing holds the focus and clarity of a formal sit-down meeting, even for basic meetings.

Here are characteristics of basic meetings:

- basic, simple, and mostly unstructured; sometimes just brief discussions on the go
- can be sufficient for small companies or start-ups with an intuitive shared perspective and close working relationship
- can have its place in larger organizations depending on the issue
- preparing for and running the meeting depend solely on the leader
- default meeting level for an inexperienced leader
- held only as needed, rather than being scheduled in advance
- tend not to include standard meeting processes or procedures (such as written agendas, note-taking, and distribution of recorded notes)

Chapter Twelve
Intermediate Meetings

INTERMEDIATE

Organizations need intermediate meetings when their growing size requires more meeting horsepower.

Moving from an unstructured meeting approach to regularly scheduled and structured meetings with clarified procedures takes effort. Companies tend to incorporate intermediate-level meetings when management responsibilities require multiple managers to pull together and when departments form within an organization. Sometimes a start-up led by an experienced founder begins at this level, because the leader knows how to start out the gate with intermediate-level meetings. Regardless, building these meetings takes work and trust among participants.

The meeting discipline of structure defines the difference between basic and intermediate meetings. Once implemented, serving leaders become competent in using a three-step meeting framework—preparing for, leading, and following up after the meeting. Leaders should educate themselves in best practices for this level of structure.

These meetings always have an agenda, a clear purpose, and written records of results. Key procedures are present, such as preparing meeting documents for better visual understanding, vetting agenda items prior to the meeting, and taking meeting notes. These procedures function as guardrails to keep each meeting focused, on track, and effective.

Delegation is key. Even if the meeting leader or chairperson is inexperienced, intermediate meetings provide enough meeting structure and process that people around the table know what's to be expected.

> **66** **When everyone is actively participating, the serving leader's job is to create an environment where every person's contribution feels valued. 99**

Country Value didn't always have intermediate meetings. Ray recalled that in the beginning, most of the meeting firepower included only the organization's two owners, Elam and his brother Jonas Esh. As a consequence, these meetings tended to address whatever was the crisis of the moment. Ray recalled, "Elam and Jonas would discuss things such as, 'The sander is broken. We've tried everything. What are we going to do about it?' It wasn't so much forward-looking, as it was focused on the here and now."

As the organization grew, however, Elam knew he would need to develop other leaders, as well as develop better meetings. Steven, the company's marketing manager, recalled that the journey of developing intermediate-level meetings started five years prior to holding management meetings on a monthly basis. "This structure wasn't documented," he said, "but we had sort of an unwritten code to follow. The president would type up a written agenda with a few key topics to discuss. We would attempt to gather shortly after lunch, but participants frequently arrived late. We then went down through the agenda items one by one, which frequently led to lengthy discussion and rabbit trailing into other areas, causing us to lose track of time, and then quickly skim other topics or not discuss them at all. There was also only a sporadic method of gathering the team's consensus. And capturing clear to-dos was hit or miss."

Steven said even their monthly meeting and covering of key topics was a big improvement over the previous method of basic-level meetings, when they met only as needed to make decisions. The largest benefit of moving to the intermediate level came when they consistently met on a monthly basis to review and implement a written agenda with discussion of initiatives. This translated into better accountability and follow-through. Even though it was only a monthly meeting, the team heard from each other, and they could act within their sphere with more knowledge of the other departments of the company.

> **" Respect is the fertile ground from which synergy can flourish. "**

At this level, the meeting disciplines of facilitation, engagement, synergy, and ownership are stepped up. An intermediate meeting with its appropriate structure now gives space for methods of simple facilitation. Leveling up looks like participants coming to the meeting prepared to engage as active participants free of distractions. When you're hanging over the fence talking to your coworker on the farm, there are no rules around engagement. When everyone is actively participating, the serving leader's job is to create an environment where every person's contribution feels valued. Respect is the fertile ground from which synergy can flourish. While participants aren't expected to own or explicitly improve the meeting (which is characteristic of an advanced meeting), everyone is there by choice and doing their part to create value in the conversation.

Another manager at Country Value said, "Over time, as the team has grown together, we've gotten livelier in discussion and in sharing opinions and thoughts." It took several years—and the help of Ray—for the company to move meetings solidly into the intermediate level. As their meetings skills improved, Elam felt them hit their stride and knew they could soon go to the next level. Their organization with forty-five employees still needed more meeting horsepower.

Here are the characteristics of intermediate meetings:

- can be sufficient in organizations with fewer than twenty-five people
- more formal than basic meetings, but generally lacking a 3D approach (meeting disciplines, types, and levels)
- known and consistent meeting guidelines and practices
- meetings adequately structured with three distinct stages: preparing, leading, and following up
- leaders holding a learn-as-you-go mindset to improve meetings, even without formally studying meeting management techniques
- structure becoming less reliant on an experienced leader, with the structure itself guiding the meeting
- increased delegation of meeting functions, such as note-taking and meeting presentations

Chapter Thirteen
Advanced Meetings

Advanced meetings are designed to bear a heavier load, and require a more systematic approach. This means leaders must have adequate training in meeting methodology. Specifically, a serving leader must understand meeting disciplines, types, and levels so they can advance. In practice, you often hit the ceiling of performance due to a lack of understanding of the principles driving an effective practice.

You may not be able to learn your way into advanced meetings alone; both Elam Esh and I needed a coach to help us learn how to lead. No one becomes an expert or reaches the advanced level that creates peak performance without knowledge and many hours of practice. Most notable is that it's not merely a matter of knowledge and skill, but ultimately it takes mature character to lead advanced meetings—influenced by the Holy Spirit. Character is often developed by rubbing shoulders with those around you, whether with your team or with a coach. Sometimes bad habits need to break; other times old ways of doing things need to be replaced. Often, leaders need those around them to give them the courage to develop what they don't yet possess.

> **" In practice, you often hit the ceiling of performance due to a lack of understanding of the principles driving an effective practice. "**

With Elam at the helm, Country Value's implementation of intermediate-level skills had drastically changed the company. As time continued, Elam and the leadership team recognized the potential for more. With the willingness to grow and the demands of the business increasing, they asked Ray to help them take their meetings to the next level.

One of their first steps to developing an advanced meeting culture was learning to understand and implement meeting types—starting with foundational meetings. After considerable debate, they chose a ninety-minute weekly management meeting as the starting point.

The first matter of business was setting ground rules around how they interacted in meetings, as well as custom-designing the structure. Instead of team members rushing in late, everybody was present several minutes before it started. Rather than mixing up reporting on projects and simultaneously discussing each, there was a clearly defined time to report and a separate time for discussion where they decided what needed to be done. Previously, in the reporting section of their meetings, people routinely wanted to give narratives on the whats and the whys. To break this habit, Elam went as far as to write in bold letters at the top of the whiteboard, "NO TANGENTS!" While this could sound extreme, Elam was convinced clear separation of reporting and discussion points was best.

Last, instead of random expectations of when a to-do was to be completed, a new approach was utilized where each to-do item was written down and verbally acknowledged at the end of the meeting with three W's—*who* will do *what* by *when*? No longer were to-do items vague statements like "Think about ideas for the paint room." Instead, action items read like: "Brainstorm with Joel and submit a report with suggestions for the paint room by Wednesday." This led to greater accountability and quicker execution, enhanced communication, and a more manageable approach to addressing issues and opportunities.

Eventually, after learning to run an advanced meeting as their weekly management meeting, Country Value also upgraded their annual strategic planning meeting to the next level. "A big learning experience has been to know what issues belong in what meeting," Elam said. "Our weekly meetings are spent on execution and improvement.

> " It's not merely a matter of knowledge and skill, but ultimately it takes mature character to lead advanced meetings—influenced by the Holy Spirit. "

On the other hand, our quarterly and annual meetings have become focused on strategy and vision. They refresh us on our long-term focus and core values." As with any meeting system being custom-designed, meetings need to be put together as an interconnected set, none existing in isolation. For example, the weekly management meeting must be viewed in light of the quarterly leadership meeting, and the quarterly leadership meeting in light of the annual strategic planning meeting.

Advanced meetings are a bit like the difference between navigating unfamiliar city streets by following a paper map versus a GPS. With the GPS, you're given clear and definitive next steps to take. You know which way you should turn before it's time to turn. In advanced meetings, the structure is intentionally designed and mapped out, providing an efficient and clear path of action, even when there are roadblocks. Just like a navigational system, if a detour is needed, there's already a route decided upon. For example, if you run out of time in a meeting, there's already a predetermined way to handle undiscussed items.

Leading meetings at an advanced level with the discipline of structure gives necessary and healthy leverage and control of the direction of the company. This gives the serving leader the tools to turn intention into action. Too many leaders turn the steering wheel of the organization, and nothing happens. It's as if the tires aren't connected to the steering

column. With the discipline of structure, the values of the company can be consistently expressed, and goals are completed as planned.

This is clearly demonstrated by the practice of great note-taking. Having structure around what gets captured (understandings, decisions, and to-dos) creates a direct line of sight to when the action will occur in the future. The magic happens when great notes are used by a leader to prepare for the next meeting, refreshing the mind on recent activity so they can lead the group further and faster.

Structure gives a steering wheel to the serving leader to create change throughout the organization—but not without great relationships guided by the disciplines of engagement and synergy. This people-centric, value-laden approach to meetings radically increases the horsepower of meetings. In such a setting, members can vet a diversity of opinions, even contentious ones, without coming to blows or becoming bitter. Crucial issues can be fully explored, and everyone can safely keep their vulnerable heart at the table.

The quality of these times of communication is guided by the discipline of facilitation. With the flow of the meeting carefully led, attendees are supported in a conversation that's alive with visual aids that spark under-standing as well as great questions to guide discussion. Advanced facil-itation intentionally creates a high sensory environment where meeting participants quickly absorb, understand, and discover information.

In preparation for writing this guide, I traveled to Pittsburgh to work through the concept with Dr. Shannah Tharp-Gilliam, an expert in edu-cational learning processes. When I walked into the room, large Post-it® notes hung on the wall with colorful markers and notecards on standby. Throughout the morning, her creative facilitation processes pulled ideas and passion out of me. Many times, she had me on my feet referencing Post-it® notes on the wall and walking around the room scanning different information. I went home with a fresh vision and a solid map for the work ahead of me.

In my experience, participants love advanced meetings because of the increased positive and measurable impact of such work. In a culture of advanced meetings, everyone takes ownership. Passive participation is disallowed. This joint ownership between leaders and their team empowers each person to raise questions and speak up—even about improving the meeting itself. Participants feel a sense of unity in working toward a common goal with others—as a "band of brothers."

Just as a ten-acre homestead doesn't need a powerful tractor, not every organization needs to conduct advanced meetings, which for smaller entities may in fact be overkill. But if your organization has outgrown the limits of intermediate meetings, it's time to level up.

Here are the characteristics of advanced meetings:

- ideal for organizations of more than twenty-five people
- leaders have a 3D mindset (meeting disciplines, types, and levels)
- characterized by full engagement, deep synergy, and rich relationships
- all participants actively own and build better meetings together
- organizational values are championed and nurtured
- leaders eager to learn and train others in higher-level meeting skills
- meetings are studied and leaders are committed to continuous improvement

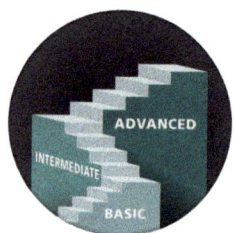

Chapter Fourteen

Leveling Up Your Meetings

How much meeting horsepower does your organization need? Any of the three levels may be appropriate, depending on your company's size, complexity, and load. Don't think of these levels as bad, better, and best. Think of them as levels of increasing horsepower that are applied depending on needs and circumstances. This framework of meeting levels helps you determine your current organizational load and to evaluate whether you need to level up. As a general rule, businesses with up to five employees can adequately operate with basic meetings. Companies with up to twenty-five people are likely served well with intermediate meetings but could benefit from adding elements of advanced meetings. Inevitably, organizations larger than twenty-five employees need the horsepower of advanced meetings.

Leveling Up Markers

Look for the telltale signs your meetings need to move up to the next level:

- Meetings are hijacked by issues that emerge but don't belong in the current meeting.
- Goals aren't clearly understood and are not completed on time.
- Resources are misaligned with work expectations, resulting in frustrated workers.
- Desired outcomes are impeded by too much chaos and disorder in meetings.
- Frequent misunderstandings happen about who's responsible for what and by when.
- Problems are rarely resolved, and quick fixes only perpetuate long-standing issues.

Leveling up is accomplished through increasing intensity of all five meeting disciplines. The very act of working to improve your meetings is meeting ownership, the fifth meeting discipline.

Making It Practical

Implementing meeting change is disruptive, but the pain of change is eased if you make it manageable in bite-size pieces. These five steps will guide you in leveling up your meetings:

1. Identify lack of meeting skills.
2. Cast a vision.
3. Choose small wins.
4. Experiment for a quarter.
5. Commit to an annual plan.

1   Step One: Identify Lack of Meeting Skills

If you want a precise measurement of your current meeting skills, take *The Serving Leader Meeting Assessment*. This scores the skills taught in this guide. Your assessment scores will immediately provide comprehensive insight and will reveal your greatest meeting strengths and weaknesses. *The Serving Leader Meeting Assessment* can be found at: http://www.servingleader.org/meeting-assessment.

Take the assessment, then have your team members individually score your meetings and combine results into a team score. Read scores aloud and verbally process the results together. Group discussion takes numbers on a page and colors in the reality behind the results of the assessment. What does a specific practice look like during meetings for your team? What meeting experience do the skills, or the lack thereof, create? Each practice has a unique bent with each meeting culture. Ask your team these questions for further evaluation:

- What are our greatest meeting strengths?
- What are our greatest meeting weaknesses?
- What skills are most important to us?
- What do we wish would change?

For further clarity on a specific score, ask, "Why did you score this skill at this number?" Ask them to give an example of instances in past meetings that prompted them to give the score. As a serving leader, remain humble as you guide this conversation.

2   Step Two: Cast a Vision

After exploratory discussion of the group's assessment results, lead the discussion towards what your meeting culture could look like in the future. Answer these questions to determine if a clear and compelling vision can be cast:

- Is there enough knowledge among team members to improve? Depending on the answers, some may want to read this guide.
- Is there sufficient interest to create a serious plan? Determining the interest level will help you form a realistic vision.

Your team's interest could lead the vision in one of three directions:

1. If interest level is low, choosing small wins (step three) will be the extent of the vision for your team. As a serving leader, you can continue to hone your own meeting skills.
2. If interest level is moderate or members are curious what meeting improvement will do for the culture, the vision will encompass choosing small wins (step three) and experimenting with improving a few skills for a quarter (step four).
3. If interest level is high, committing to an annual journey of improving meeting skills (step five), starting with choosing

small wins (step three), and selecting a few skills to work on for the first quarter (step four) will shape the vision.

Once you choose a direction for your team, paint a picture of what the future will look like on the other side of achieving the vision. Articulate the outcome, particularly the reversal of what's been holding your meetings back. Talk about what's at stake if you don't achieve the vision. Imagine together what the result will be.

3 Step Three: Choose Small Wins

The best place to start improving your meetings is with low hanging fruit—the quick win. Take note of the easy things discovered in this guide that you could change about your meetings. These changes should be clear no-brainers to implement. What you choose should be something you easily understand and can run with, feeling both confident and competent.

> " *This feeling of a quick win will give your team the momentum to tackle the bigger, and likely tougher, meeting changes that are needed.* "

For example, if the leader of the discussions has also been keeping track of the time or taking notes, simply assign someone else to do it. If weather is the topic of choice to transition into a meeting, share a story that aligns with the values of the company instead. These small changes will make a big difference. This feeling of a quick win will give your team the momentum to tackle the bigger, and likely tougher, meeting changes that are needed. Continue the practice of these small changes until your next quarterly meeting.

4 Step Four: Experiment for a Quarter

After your team has experienced a handful of positive meeting changes, discuss the details of your meeting skills experiment. During the quarterly meeting, take the answers from the questions "What skills are most important to us?" and "What do we wish would change?" and choose three to five skills to work on for the next ninety days. Consider using the wording of the skill in the assessment to make the goal of improvement clear.

Next, once you've identified no more than five meeting skills, gather the team's resources and begin to direct your energy toward your current meetings. Such effort may be best spread out across various team members by a member accepting the challenge to effect change on a particular meeting skill within their ability to do so. This is taking ownership, as described in chapter 7.

Incorporate these meeting skills as part of a regular, recurring meeting agenda discussion item. To get fresh perspective on progress, use the last two to three minutes of the meeting to reap participants' feedback and advice for improvements. Adjust accordingly.

Focusing on improving these skills tends to feel hard because the change requires a renovation of what's been the norm. These types of changes could drastically impact your company culture and will take time. Because of the grip of habits, you may serve your team best by getting a coach. Think of improving meetings in the way a runner trains for a long-distance race. Increasing endurance and speed takes knowledge, planning, and practice.

> " The blood, sweat, and tears involved in the practice of these skills will bring the transformation of character every serving leader commits to when choosing the path of life-giving meetings. "

 ## Step Five: Commit to an Annual Plan

Leveling up requires time and commitment and can easily take a year of concerted effort to move from one meeting level to the next. Depending on the buy-in of your team, you may start with an annual focus on improvement. If your team wanted to experiment first, the group may decide after a quarter whether to continue for a year of meeting skill improvement.

Improving a dozen meeting skills is roughly equivalent to moving up a level. A longer commitment will be in order if you've identified your team's need as being a level higher than your current one. Occasionally a

Illustration 17: Serving leaders discipline themselves to steadily improve their meeting skills.

company needs to focus on a few large or difficult skills to solidify their footing on a particular level.

Recently, I handed out *The Serving Leader Meeting Assessment* to my team of five direct reports with whom I meet biweekly. The assessment results created a significant conversation and birthed vision to improve our meetings, even though we're running mostly advanced-level meetings. Out of the assessment results, we then chose two meeting skills to improve and set them as a quarterly goal. When a company is operating at a lower horsepower than needed, leveling up requires a dozen or more skills—renovating the way they meet.

With the insight of *The Serving Leader Meeting Assessment* and a courageous team by your side, one foot in front of the other climbing the meeting steps will bring you closer to your next level (see illustration 17). Committing to the discipline of ownership and improving your meetings will transform your meeting culture. The blood, sweat, and tears involved in the practice of these skills will bring the transformation of character every serving leader commits to when choosing the path of life-giving meetings.

Chapter Fifteen
Tying It All Together

*Everybody ends up somewhere in life. A few people
end up somewhere on purpose.*

ANDY STANLEY

Likely you're inspired with fresh insights and vision to stop participating in what Patrick Lencioni calls "death by meeting." With this guide, you have a wealth of knowledge on how to lead life-giving meetings. However, obtaining knowledge isn't the same as achieving practical skills informed by that knowledge. Most leaders lack the discipline and coaching to implement what they already know.

After my wake-up call where my partners took me to task, I got serious about improving meetings, but it took me several years to gain the significant transformation I needed. As Ray's coaching helped me break my old meeting habits, they were replaced by new ones. My meeting journey continues, and I remain a work in progress.

This guide is your coach bringing to your doorstep concepts from the experts on meetings. More importantly, you heard practical advice from ordinary business leaders like Elam from Country Value Woodworks as he learned to lead better meetings. Reaching the ceiling of meetings is not merely mastering the five disciplines of meetings, nor developing the right set of meeting types, nor even leveling up to the next level of meeting horsepower. Instead, the ceiling limit is often a matter of character.

Leading life-giving meetings is unlike a physical sport, where improvement can be achieved by merely training human muscles through practice. Life-giving meetings require the training of *spiritual* muscles. Jesus said it succinctly, "I came that they may have life and have it abundantly" (John 10:10). This abundant life is experienced when human character is shaped and forged through the indwelling, life-giving Spirit of God. It then permeates and transforms our beliefs and desires with truth and love until it is finally expressed through renewed behaviors, attitudes, and practices.

The five disciplines of this guide are mysteriously hard to achieve if the presence of the Spirit, with the aid of others, has not yet forged your character. Ultimately, without the life-giving Spirit of God acting in concert with a serving leader's character, many meeting skills are elusive. For this reason, I've included in the appendix a chapter on *The Serving Leader Model*. After all, this guide is written from a Christian worldview—a serving approach to meetings, not merely a guide with five effective meeting disciplines. As such, if Christ is not present in meetings and has not transformed your character, expect death by meeting.

Growing up in the Christian Anabaptist culture, I experienced the blessing of tradition at the close of many worship services. The minister would end with the following prayer: "Now to him who is able to do far more abundantly than all that we ask or think, according to the power at work within us" (Ephesians 3:20). With my eyes closed, those gripping words brought hope to my soul seeking strength for life. Yet I seldom saw this "power at work within" my own experience to be in abundant supply. More often than not, I wanted much more from the Lord than I was experiencing. As I grew into leadership, this became even more pronounced.

I experienced disappointment because I assumed this power at work within me was mysteriously available upon sincere request. What I didn't realize in my naivete, that is it's far more complicated than that.

Consider that tapping the power within is not merely claiming Christ's power in a moment of need. As an example, leaders can abdicate their leadership and pray quietly for God to rescue them during an intense moment of a meeting—in vain. Imagine the difference if the leader embraced the road less traveled of Christ transforming their character and honing their ability and emotional wisdom to lead a difficult conversation. In this sense, the power within comes long before the moment of crisis—through character formation, shaped through suffering, weakness, and lowliness.

Experiencing the power within for sure isn't believing in yourself or just trusting your heart. It's not only embracing Biblical principles or practicing until perfection. Many great Christians struggle hard with good intentions to serve the Lord, longing to find the power to live out their lives—in this case, lead meetings. Their desire is for daily practical power on the ground. This is not found in relying on miraculous moments or a firm commitment to just do the right thing. How does one do the right thing without the necessary internal infrastructure to do so? This infrastructure includes a Christian worldview, a humbled heart forged through suffering, and practical knowledge about the world, all of which translates into a developed character infused with the Spirit. Simply opening the meeting with a prayer or being intentional about doing the right thing will not drive your meeting dysfunction away.

When the human and divine converge, transforming our character, the power at work inside us begins to grow beyond the common grace of human beliefs, desires, and skills. Walk the long road of transformation with the Lord and take the critiques and encouragement from those around you. Then, and only then, will leaders develop their character, principles, desires, and skills beyond the human level of common grace. This will require a thorough dose of sacrifice, weakness, and humility and is a lifelong process. If you want the inner power to lead effective meetings, you will find it in abundant supply on the far side of suffering, searching, learning, and practicing—with Christ and His followers.

> " Imagine the difference if the leader embraced the road less traveled of Christ transforming their character and honing their ability and emotional wisdom to lead a difficult conversation. "

Step-by-Step Guides

Chapter Sixteen

The Weekly Management Meeting Guide

The truth is, there is no more valuable activity in any organization than the regular staff meeting of a leadership team. But if they are not effective, there is little or no chance of building a cohesive team or a healthy organization.

PATRICK LENCIONI, *The Advantage*

The rhythmic meetings of a management or leadership team are a staple in any company. The goal of the weekly management meeting is to share important information, drive accountability, and resolve issues to maintain momentum. The weekly agenda is structured to address the company's top priorities that are set in the quarterly and annual meetings. Held at the same time on the same day every week, this is a tactical hands-on working meeting. Leading it effectively rests largely on developing strong relationships within the team and following a specific structure.

This meeting is also different from a weekly team meeting of employees or an all-staff meeting. However, such meetings may follow some of the same structure. In some situations, this management meeting can be held once every two weeks and still accomplish the goal. Whether the leadership team meets weekly or biweekly depends on factors such as the competency of the leaders, the weight of responsibility they bear, the complexity of the product or service, and current market conditions. As you grow your meeting skills and adopt a systematized approach to meetings, the biweekly approach can become more viable, especially if you have a small team that stays well-connected. For example, in two of the organizations for which I serve on the management team, we use a weekly structure with the freedom to skip a week if a meeting isn't needed. Typically, we cancel one or two weekly meetings per quarter. At my own company, AgSalt Processing, we use the biweekly approach.

Preparing for the Meeting

Good preparation is often the best predictor of a great outcome. Good preparation for a weekly management meeting requires five steps:

1. Plan the logistics.
2. Design the agenda.
3. Prepare the documents and resources.

4. Send the meeting invitation and agenda.
5. Prepare the participants and meeting space.

 Step One: Plan the Logistics

Consistency in the schedule is key to establishing an effective rhythm. Pick a day, time, and location for the meeting each week and stick with it for at least a quarter. Consistent scheduling enables leaders to plan out months in advance and reserve their calendars for the weekly meeting.

Decide on a chairperson who will run the meeting and lead the team through the agenda. Designate a second person to take notes and keep track of time. Splitting meeting management into two roles avoids overloading the chairperson and frees them up to lead. From time to time, consider changing up these roles among participants to develop their facilitation skills.

 Step Two: Design the Agenda

As part of the consistent rhythm of this meeting, use the same basic agenda each week, and simply update the reporting items and discussion points. Use a template (see table 1) to keep the agenda preparation from becoming a monumental task.

The chairperson must seek input from team members and establish the discussion points for the upcoming meeting. These points should be determined roughly one day in advance. First, check for issues from the previous week which were tabled due to time restraints. If a tabled item is

> **"As a serving leader, think ahead about what your team needs to enable them to fully understand the issues and to engage in the discussion."**

ready for discussion, add it to the agenda. Screen your discussion points, guarding against items that are too big or small for the weekly meeting. If a discussion point is too large, it will hijack the other important items, thus deserving its own dedicated meeting. On the other hand, avoid spending time on tiny issues that should be handled in a side conversation. Some points—which are information only and don't need a discussion—may be small enough to share at the beginning of the meeting.

After the discussion points are determined, but prior to the meeting, the chairperson should list the discussion points in order of best sequence or order of importance according to their perspective. The discussion order will then be finalized in the meeting by the team. If possible, list the items as a question to be answered. For example, instead of listing "Approve product design," write, "Are we moving forward with design one, two, or three?" Assign each discussion point to the person responsible to present it. Finally, if a discussion point needs a specific facilitation method, make sure the person responsible is prepared to use it. For example, they may have three questions to guide the conversation or a sketch on the whiteboard to facilitate brainstorming.

Step Three: Prepare the Documents and Resources

The meeting chairperson is responsible for determining whether any agenda items need preparation in advance. Serve your team by helping them avoid the situation of someone walking into a meeting while still scrambling to pull together documents then running to the printer to grab papers. As a serving leader, think ahead about what your team needs to enable them to fully understand the issues and engage in the discussion. Often it's helpful to have the key points and information presented visually, whether in a document or on a whiteboard or projector.

> **" Keep the focus on weekly functions and day-to-day issues so you don't veer off into visionary or strategy discussions. "**

Each meeting should include a quick performance review, backed by numbers. These numbers (often called key performance indicators or KPIs) should be compiled into a weekly scorecard or dashboard prior to the meeting. This data can be collected in several different ways. You could designate one person to update the numbers every week or assign specific metrics to different people. You could also use a collaborative approach with a shared document editor so everyone can update the data simultaneously.

Some small organizations do not track weekly KPIs. Instead, managers have their fingers on the pulse of their departments and have a gut sense of productivity. This approach can be sufficient for some small companies, but even small companies will find that tracking and reporting productivity brings increased clarity.

Step Four: Send the Meeting Invitation and Agenda

At least a half-day in advance, send the finalized agenda and any supporting documents to everyone attending. This will ensure participants can read background materials and prepare their initial thoughts ahead of time.

Step Five: Prepare the Participants and Meeting Space

During this preparation time, participants should make sure all meeting data is updated. They can add last-minute discussion points and reflect on what they're grateful for or on important information to share with the team. Arriving with no forethought is a recipe for a mediocre meeting.

The chairperson and secretary are a mini team both before and during the meeting. Be clear about who does what in prep work. If printed documents are used, typically the secretary is responsible to provide every team member with copies at each seat. They also are often responsible for setting up the space in a way that's conducive to productivity.

There's no reason to stumble at the starting line of meetings. The old adage remains true: "By failing to prepare, you're preparing to fail."

> **" Being fully present means focusing your emotions and mental attention on others, coupled with presenting yourself as ready and open to engage in relational experiences. "**

Leading the Meeting

Meeting structure is your friend as a leader. As you lead, keep in mind that the weekly management meeting is operational and tactical. Keep the focus on weekly functions and day-to-day issues (administrative, operational, and personnel) so you don't veer off into visionary or strategy discussions.

This agenda requires discipline to pack seven important steps into sixty to ninety minutes of high impact discussion. Each step has a suggested time limit.

Follow these guidelines to conduct the meeting efficiently and effectively:

- Start and end the meeting on time. Prioritize the discussion points and keep the least important points last. If you run out of time, they can be tabled for a later meeting.
- Separate reporting from discussion.
- Use effective questions to deepen discussion and draw out better ideas.
- Use a meeting timer for effective time management.

The meeting notes should be recorded directly under each discussion point in the order of discussion. All points should have a note in the form of an understanding, a decision, or a to-do. To-dos should be listed separately from the discussion points. Move unaddressed discussion points, along with those chosen to be discussed later, to the tabled section of the notes. This step ensures that everyone has a record of what happened and of their next action steps. Not only does documentation give your team the best chance for success, but it creates a culture of accountability from which a serving leader can effectively support the team.

AGENDA SEGMENT	ACTIVITY	DURATION
Get Present and Personal	Eliminate distractions and engage others with eye contact; share a personal item.	5–10 minutes
Important Information	Share important information too small to be a discussion point.	10 minutes
Dashboard	Review key performance indicators.	5 minutes
Quarterly Goals	Review the company's quarterly goals.	5 minutes
Previous Week's To-Dos	Review previous week's list of to-dos.	5 minutes
Discussion Points	As necessary, arrange discussion points in best sequential order; prioritize top three issues; set a time for each discussion point; discuss, debate, and decide.	20–50 minutes
Wrap-Up	Recap major decisions; read aloud assigned to-dos; record tabled issues or discussion points; coordinate any necessary communication to the rest of the organization; rate the meeting on a scale of 1–10.	10 minutes

Table 1: Example of a weekly management meeting agenda.

It's important to custom design your meetings to fit your unique needs. For example, maybe reporting dashboard numbers isn't relevant for you. Adjust these steps to fit your needs.

 ## Step One: Get Present and Personal

Getting present is not rushing into the meeting and arriving just in time. It's showing up with your head, heart, and body completely focused on the other participants. Being fully present means focusing your emotions and mental attention on others, coupled with presenting yourself as ready and open to engage in relational experiences. It's pushing aside distractions and honoring others through eye contact and facial expressions that communicate genuine delight in being with them. This first few minutes of welcoming banter and goodwill sets the precedent for a people-centric meeting culture.

Beyond the lively chitchat of gathering around the table, everyone gets personal with a brief, meaningful time of sharing about their lives. This step is important because sharing creates a fresh connection and a sense of camaraderie, building trust and relational equity for the discussion to follow. Getting personal as a group could end in a prayer or a scripture reading as a powerful form of inviting God's presence into the meeting.

 ## Step Two: Share Important Information and Values

This second step of the meeting shifts directly into the weekly information and news that matter to those around the table. What you share and value will highlight what's important to your team culture.

The key is sharing tidbits of information that help participants stay in tune with each other's area of work. These bite-size points or tidbits of news should be too small to be considered a discussion item, but can become so if more discussion is needed. Examples include employee, customer, or vendor news or stories and event information. It can also include the key tasks of a person's week that intersect with another manager's.

Recently in one of the companies I lead, we had skipped our previous weekly meeting, so there were more tidbits than usual. In five minutes, the various department managers fired off about ten interesting happenings, including filling me in on an employee going-away party that I missed. This sort of rapid-fire delivery of information keeps the management team informed and connected to areas of the organization they don't monitor.

> " A weekly alignment check comparing weekly progress against quarterly goals is a surefire way to hit them. "

Appreciation and gratitude reinforce organizational values. This is the place in the meeting to talk about how a team member demonstrated a core value of the company during the week. This is a powerful way to reinforce what your company stands for and to develop a strong culture.

Step Three: Report Dashboard Numbers

Key performance indicators quantify organizational performance at a glance. Weekly performance should be compared to a target number that's an efficient benchmark of progress.

When using KPIs, assign managers to report on numbers within their sphere of operations. If the KPI is off target, evaluate the negative trend to determine whether there's a need for discussion. If so, drop it to the discussion portion of the meeting to limit this part of the meeting to reporting.

Step Four: Report on Quarterly Goals

This fourth step assumes that you set quarterly goals and treat the weekly meeting as a subset of quarterly leadership plans. This step is vital, because a weekly alignment check comparing weekly progress against quarterly goals is a surefire way to hit them.

Each quarterly goal should be owned by a specific person and should be briefly stated as either "on track" or "off track" and no more. If a goal needs discussion or problem-solving, put it on the list of discussion points.

As with any step, customize this one to meet your needs. For example, in my department at Anabaptist Financial, we review quarterly goals once a month instead of weekly. But at AgSalt Processing, we maintain a sharper focus, reminding ourselves weekly of our quarterly goals. Either rhythm can work.

5 Step Five: Report on the Previous Week's To-Dos

To-dos are tasks or actions that arise as a result of a discussion or decision. Reporting on written to-dos or action items from the previous week's meeting is the most effective method to drive performance with accountability. This critical step enables each team member to give account to the group on their weekly progress without lengthy explanations.

In this step, read the previous week's to-dos, with each team member responding with "complete" or "incomplete." As a general rule, aim for 80 percent or more completion of to-dos by your team each week. A to-do item shouldn't be on the list for more than two weeks. If discussion is needed around an incomplete item, move it to the discussion portion of the meeting. This step answers the questions of "What has been done?" and "What still needs to be done?"

6 Step Six: Prioritize and Talk Through Discussion Points

Discussion points are the heart of the weekly meeting. It takes by far the largest block of time, in contrast to the brief reporting segment. A discussion point represents a challenge, an insight, or a question that relates to running the business operationally.

> " The serving leader's job is to guide the discussion, ensuring that everyone's opinion is represented. "

This part of the meeting involves discussing, deepening understanding around issues, and making decisions. Start by asking if any additional talking points need to be added to the list. This could include adding things that came up during the reporting part of the meeting or last-minute issues brought to the table.

Next, prioritize the discussion points, listing the most important topics first but sequencing to protect meeting flow. Choose the top three to five issues. To make this go fast, the chairperson should have previously arranged the list in order of importance. But give a minute for others to reorder the list, if necessary. Keep the length of the list realistic. As Tim Cook says, "The longer the meeting, the less is accomplished."

The serving leader's job is to guide the discussion, ensuring that everyone's opinion is represented. The discussion must be led toward one of the following four conclusions: an understanding, a decision, a to-do, or tabling the issue.

Some issues may require two meetings, allowing for further research or time to sleep on it. If it becomes apparent that the issue will require more work than will fit inside the weekly meeting, push the issue to a separate problem-solving meeting or some other type of meeting.

Many leaders find that wrapping up the discussion on time is the most difficult part of keeping a meeting disciplined. To better manage this segment of the meeting, consider asking the presenter of the point for a time allotment as they begin. This helps the presenter to be time conscious. Also consider the use of a meeting timer with remaining time highly visible.

 ### Step Seven: Wrap Up the Meeting

All meetings are brought to an effective close through a four-point review.

First, decisions and to-dos should be verbally recapped and affirmed. Review to-dos and ensure that each task is assigned to a specific person with a deadline.

Second, ask if any item came to mind throughout the meeting that should be tabled or put on the list for the next time.

Third, ask whether any information discussed needs to be communicated to anyone outside of the meeting. If so, assign a to-do.

Finally, consider reflecting how you could improve in the future. If an aspect of the conversation was difficult, ask for feedback. This could include having participants rate it on a scale of 1–10 or sharing how they're feeling about the meeting.

Ending on time should be a priority, because it promotes a consistent and efficient meeting culture. Effectively wrapping up is important for clarity and closure.

Following Up after the Meeting

Be aware that a meeting well-conducted can turn into a disappointment because something wasn't documented, and participants' memories fade in the whirlwind of daily work and urgent tasks. When you follow up well, you break the finish line tape in full stride.

 ### Step One: Publish Meeting Notes

The secretarial role includes sending the notes and to-dos within a few hours of the meeting. These are sent to all attendees as well as any team member who couldn't attend. Providing great follow-up is one more way to serve and equip your team, because they count on the meeting notes and to-dos to guide their actions.

Step Two: Reflect on the Meeting

Some of the best breakthrough ideas come after the discussion. Be prepared to capture your afterthoughts by submitting them to the secretary and attaching them as an addendum. If the breakthrough idea is a game changer, consider convening a special meeting.

Reflect on your leadership during the course of the meeting. Self-awareness leads to growth. Reflect on others and how they responded to determine whether further comments or discussion would be helpful. What you observe can be a talking point for a more private discussion or simply a later conversation like a one-on-one meeting. These reflections can be the key to improving your meetings and relationships one step at a time.

 ## Step Three: Complete To-Dos

Teams feel frustrated when great decisions are made but no follow-through occurs or when tasks are committed to but not completed on time. Unfortunately, this is all too common. This is one reason why it's important to document follow-up actions in written to-dos. If you manage a task list in one place, be sure to transfer your action items from the meeting. As a serving leader, demonstrate credibility by always completing your to-dos on time.

Following up on the meeting can be difficult, even anticlimactic. These steps can feel like boring details compared to the meeting itself. It's paramount, however, to finish the race. Small steps taken by your team every week will lead to big results in your organization.

Finally, if you're determined to transform your meetings, be prepared to feel personal internal resistance as well as some pushback from your team. Change is rarely the easy path forward, but you can be the courageous serving leader who takes that transformative step.

Chapter Seventeen
The Direct Report One-on-One Meeting Guide

One-on-ones once a week are the single greatest tool to raise people up through the ranks.

DANIEL WENGERD

A serving leader is always on the lookout for better ways to connect with and lead their people. The practice of having regular, structured one-on-one meetings with direct reports recurs in management books and training. In my opinion, Mark Horstman's book *The Effective Manager* provides the deepest insight into this practice that may seem innovative but is actually well-established.

If you have several direct reports, spending a good part of your day in one-on-one meetings may feel like an inefficient use of your time. It's not. Horstman's research shows that one-on-one meetings pay off, literally. He studied a number of companies over a period of years and found that the practice of doing weekly, thirty- to forty-five-minute one-on-ones actually increased profit per employee compared to similar companies in the same industry that didn't do one-on-ones. We all know that investing personal interest and time in a relationship causes it to flourish. Who would have guessed that profit per employee would also increase!

> " It shouldn't surprise us that when employees feel loved and cared for at work, their motivation soars, thus impacting the bottom line. "

As serving leaders, the profit motive is secondary to the people motive. In fact, if profit is your primary motive in implementing one-on-ones, then don't even bother. It makes merchandise and mockery of the treasure of deeper relationship. Yet it shouldn't surprise us that when employees feel loved and cared for at work, their motivation soars, thus impacting the bottom line.

Non-serving leaders often take the position that employees' personal lives don't matter. Even Henry Ford complained, "Why is it every time I ask for a pair of hands, they come with a brain attached?" Another assumption is to believe that church leaders, not business leaders, are the ones responsible for people's personal lives. But to believe so requires people to compartmentalize their lives with Monday work separate from Sunday worship. One-on-ones provide a great place to invite personal and work issues to converge.

> **"** If time for one-on-one meetings isn't set aside regularly, issues naturally get swept under the rug, or they pop up and take many little inefficient discussions. **"**

Here's the hard part. I aspire to be that serving leader known for a personal touch and care. Despite my best intentions, however, I found it surprisingly difficult to learn the ropes of effective one-on-ones. Not only are they so personal that it's easy to mess them up, but I often felt too busy to take the time. As I grew into management, I relied on unstructured on-the-go types of one-on-ones. If my reports needed me, they could grab me for quick conversations when they needed it, or we would talk when I stopped by their workstations to check in on them. Because I was an unstructured sort of leader, I thought these impromptu meetings worked well. However, I learned that I could do much better.

The Purpose Behind Regular One-on-Ones

The purpose of checking in with a weekly one-on-one meeting with those who report to you is to empower them to succeed, whether professionally or personally. The goals of getting together are to build the relationship, discuss issues, and allow the direct report to give account.

First and foremost, face-to-face interaction creates the space needed to build trust and deepen relational synergy. As the leader listens and discusses the direct report's concerns and interests, this leads to knowing each other far better over time than in a group setting. These insights lead to more connection between two people and change group dynamics as the serving leader leads with more knowledge of each individual. As trust develops, more breakthrough is possible with issues and individual growth.

Second, one-on-one meetings provide a regular place to discuss issues that matter to both parties. If this time isn't set aside regularly, issues naturally get swept under the rug, or they pop up and take many little inefficient discussions. By having this space to sniff out early warning signs of trouble brewing, the leader is able to deal with obstacles and difficulties early. Often these private discussions create safety that isn't found in a group setting. This regular time helps them think through, strategize, and process work issues individually under the serving leader's mentorship with the conversation uniquely tailored to them. This develops the whole person.

Third, time set aside with your direct report increases their capacity to get things done while increasing their ability to bear responsibility. Instead of the stiff, cold approach of leaders "holding people accountable" for tasks, these meetings provide the opportunity for the direct report to "give account." This reversal of the report giving account versus the leader holding accountable honors the dignity of a person and fosters self-directed responsibility. While the leader provides the structure of the meeting up front, the direct report owns their meeting. This provides opportunity to bring up what they feel is important. When issues come up, this space gives the serving leader a place to give feedback and coaching on issues that would be inappropriate to address in a group.

The overarching purpose of one-on-ones is to build trust, develop the whole person, and increase capacity. One-on-ones send a bold statement: "You're important to me." Unfortunately, leaders often send the opposite message. Horstman writes, "If you don't schedule weekly One on Ones, you're saying to your directs, 'This might be important in a given week. You might be important, and the time with me might be valuable to me. I don't know. Let's play it by ear. We'll see how things go.'"[16]

Types of Direct Report One-on-One Meetings

I suggest four types of one-on-one meetings with those who report to you. Know the difference and customize them to your situation:

1. on-the-go meetings
2. weekly meetings
3. quarterly meetings
4. annual job review

On-the-Go Meetings: On-the-go meetings are unscheduled and pop up as the need arises. They rarely include a written agenda

or note-taking. These impromptu meetings are often less than fifteen minutes. They may include a quick stop by the workstation or a quick phone call to strike the anvil while it's hot to clarify, solve, or assist with whatever task is at hand. Brevity and efficiency are their trademark.

Despite their value, on-the-go meetings can be overused if your direct report is frequently resorting to them due to a lack of direction and the absence of weekly one-on-one meetings. For a serving leader, I don't recommend on-the-go meetings as a substitute for a weekly sit-down one-on-one because you and your report will never build the foundation of a solid relationship without those deeper conversations made possible with the quality time of weekly one-on-ones. However, being available for brief on-the-go conversations is priceless.

Weekly Meetings: Weekly one-one-ones are scheduled with each direct report. This replaces the need to rely only on impromptu conversations when circumstances require it. Typically thirty to sixty minutes in length, they are often a bit informal even though they are structured and scheduled. Weekly one-on-ones encourage developing high-trust relationships. They may address personal or work issues, and can include to-dos to keep accountability high. This deep investment in people may strike you as overkill, but it's the servant way! The results will speak for themselves.

Quarterly Meetings: One-on-ones may include certain activities that are monthly or quarterly. For example, once a quarter, a weekly one-on-one may be dedicated to setting quarterly goals with your report. At Pioneer Equipment, they set goals with each direct report once a quarter and then track the goals through the weekly one-on-ones.

Annual Job Review: The annual job review is the culmination of direct report one-on-one meetings, representing all the other one-on-one meetings throughout the year. Unlike the usual get-togethers, this is a big-picture meeting that doesn't concern itself with day-to-day tasks and discussions. The serving leader's purpose in this meeting is to reflect on and celebrate the previous year of service and to look ahead towards the next year. This once-a-year meeting takes more time. Topics covered during this type of one-on-one include employee satisfaction, job fit, and how you can support their growth and goals.

Each of these types of direct report one-on-one meetings has a unique function that intersects with the others and together produces a bond of respect between the serving leader and the report. In this guide, I will focus specifically on the weekly one-on-one meeting.

Preparing for the Meeting

Preparation for a one-on-one meeting could include five steps:

1. Plan the logistics.
2. Design the agenda.
3. Prepare the documents and resources.
4. Send the meeting invitation and agenda.
5. Prepare the participant and meeting space.

 ### Step One: Plan the Logistics

Schedule weekly one-on-ones on the calendar as a recurring event. Your reports understand that you're busy, but if they know they have your attention on a regular, dependable basis, they can count on their questions getting answered, their problems solved, and their ideas heard. Horstman says, "When you tell your direct reports that they're going to have scheduled time with you every week, no matter what, you elevate their importance to that of the rest of the items on your calendar; that is, you are making them also 'important.'"[17]

Should your one-on-ones be weekly or biweekly? Horstman's data is clear; however, I like biweekly one-on-ones because my direct reports are also managers. With our schedule of a biweekly management meeting, one week I meet with the management team; and the next week I meet with each team member individually. This puts me in touch with all my reports on a weekly basis.

> **" Your employees are your most valuable asset—despite the fact they don't appear on your balance sheet. "**

At Seven Oaks Landscaping, Galen Layman oversees operations and has implemented these one-on-ones at the ground level. He has four foremen with whom he meets individually on a weekly basis. They have set a consistent time when these one-on-ones take place. These foremen, in turn, offer the same one-on-ones to the men under them.

"If one-on-ones are not weekly," Galen says, "then it becomes once every three weeks, and then once a month, then once a quarter until, boom, it's gone."

Before Seven Oaks began to implement these one-on-one meetings, there was no set time for an employee to sit down and share with their manager or supervisor. There was a lot of on-the-go, informal interaction where the loudest, most opinionated employees were heard the most, while the quieter employees would be lost in the noise. In weekly one-on-ones, those rarely heard finally found their voice.

An employee said it this way: "We have a voice and time dedicated to express our viewpoints. Sometimes, we just talk about life. Some weeks we don't talk about work much. Instead, we just talk about family." With scheduled one-on-ones, stay within your time boundaries. If more time is needed, schedule an extra meeting.

You may be thinking, "I'm already maxed out! I can't imagine finding the time to do one-on-ones with my direct reports!" This is a common objection of busy leaders who have not yet realized that leadership is the art of growing and guiding others and that meetings are one of the best tools for that. Such leaders still believe that working *in* the business is more important than working *on* the business. Your employees are your most valuable asset—despite the fact they don't appear on your balance sheet. People feel valued when they have your ear once a week. You cannot push people to the side until it's convenient and expect them to feel trusted and valued. Keep in mind that you'll most likely gain time because one-on-ones reduce the need for on-the-go conversations.

Every person matters; spending time with each person affirms his or her value. It often takes five to ten minutes to settle into a quality conversation and another fifteen to twenty minutes to really listen and understand the

AGENDA SEGMENT	ACTIVITY	DURATION
Get Present and Personal	Eliminate distractions and engage with eye contact; share a personal item.	5–10 minutes
Important Information	Share important information too small to be a discussion point	5 minutes
Quarterly Goals	Review progress towards personal quarterly goals.	5 minutes
Previous Week's To-Dos	Review any to-dos from previous week.	5 minutes
Discussion Points	As necessary, arrange discussion points in best sequential order; prioritize top three issues; set a time for each discussion point; listen and discuss.	20–50 minutes
Wrap-Up	Recap any major decisions; read aloud assigned to-dos; record tabled issues or discussion points; share a highlight of the meeting.	5 minutes

Table 2: Example of a direct report one-on-one meeting agenda.

issues, ask clarifying questions, and offer meaningful insight. If you don't allow enough time for vulnerable communication from the heart to the surface, people won't talk about the deeper things. For these reasons, I suggest a minimum of thirty minutes for employees with less responsibility and up to sixty minutes with employees carrying heavy management loads. On that note, I suggest that a manager never has more than seven reports. If they use thirty minutes per report, this keeps one-on-ones to a half-day a week.

 Step Two: Design the Agenda

Part of your job as a serving leader is to convey your meeting expectations to your reports so they too can be prepared. When it comes to what gets addressed during the meeting, set an agenda that gives structure to each one-on-one but lets them populate the agenda for each meeting, then add anything you want to discuss afterwards. See table 2 for a flexible agenda template that can be tweaked to suit your needs and style.

 Step Three: Prepare the Documents and Resources

Although not as commonly needed in this type of meeting, make sure to have supporting documents or resources if a discussion point would benefit from such.

 Step Four: Send the Meeting Invitation and Agenda

Have your direct report send out a meeting reminder with the agenda a day before your time together.

 Step Five: Prepare the Participant and Meeting Space

One-on-ones should be personal and practical. Consider meeting on their turf or in an environment within their comfort zone. If the employee needs a casual meeting in their workspace to be comfortable, design it that way. Get a stool, enter their space, and listen to them.

On the other hand, if someone is comfortable coming to your office, that's fine too. Convey warmth and openness by putting yourself on equal footing with them. This could look like getting out from behind your desk and grabbing a coffee or pulling up a chair next to them.

Leading the Meeting

Leading the meeting is not the same as designing the meeting. Without question, the leader must design it. However, either the report or the manager can lead the meeting. As I lead my managers, I require them to lead our one-on-one meetings and take the notes. This develops them as they in turn lead one-on-ones with their reports. Depending on the level of confidence of your report, go slowly and lead the meetings until they become comfortable, then let them lead.

Take notes throughout. Don't skip this, even if it seems unnecessary in a meeting of two people. I suggest taking notes with pen and paper on each corresponding point of the printed agenda, not on a digital device that holds many distractions. Make a note of the concluding understandings, the agreed upon to-dos, and if any decisions were made or tabled for further discussion. Every discussion point on the agenda should conclude with a note along one of those four lines.

 Step One: Get Present and Personal

One-on-ones provide a unique opportunity to get past the small talk and make space for deeper discussion and even deeper disclosure of your real self. Getting present is not the same as transitioning into a meeting. The concept of getting present is a spiritual act of honoring another by presenting yourself with full attention, focus, and concentration out of respect for the other person. Getting personal is not characterized by weightless conversation about the weather or sports or some similar form of an icebreaker.

> **" Something as simple as a heartfelt 'Good morning! I'm glad to be with you!' can be powerful. "**

Instead, getting personal is offering your presence and welcoming the other person with delight and joy. A welcoming, smiling face, sparkling eyes, and open body posture along with a verbal expression of pleasure in being there all convey presence. Even something as simple as a heartfelt "Good morning! I'm glad to be with you!" can be powerful.

 Step Two: Share Important Information

Being aware of what's going on in your organization is the start of decision-making. During this segment of the meeting, listen to what is going on with your employee. Ask key questions like, "What updates do you have for me?[18] What tidbits of information are important for me to know? What happened in the last week that is important to you?"

The key is to elicit small pieces of information—which can be stated in one minute or less— but are crucial despite their brevity. These little details are often your best path to the issues that matter. A myriad of small glimpses from your report adds up to three-dimensional vision.

It will take practice for your report to distinguish between important tidbits of information that need your attention and those that don't. Highlight and affirm what you want to see more of, and they will soon learn the difference. Occasionally, a tidbit leads to a "land mine" (big problem) or the opposite, a "gold mine" (something to celebrate) that would never have surfaced otherwise.

Once, a report happened to mention that he placed an order for custom-built parts at Yoder's Industries and a delay in the shipment was holding up a repair. This revealed a misunderstanding of who did what because I happened to know that someone else had ordered the same custom-built parts at another shop. This is an example of how a tidbit may prove to be unexpectedly valuable.

Last, be quick to identify when a piece of information needs to be a discussion point. Don't hijack this section of the meeting by turning a tidbit into a five-minute discussion. Simply say, "This needs to be discussed more thoroughly. Let's move it down to the discussion segment," if you cross the minute threshold and the point still needs more time.

Note: This step is optional and can be eliminated if you share other meetings with this report where important info is shared on a weekly basis, such as in the weekly management meeting.

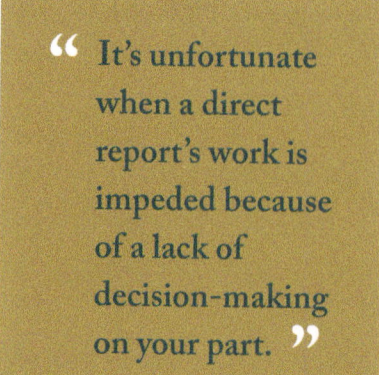

> **It's unfortunate when a direct report's work is impeded because of a lack of decision-making on your part.** "

3 Step Three: Report on Quarterly Goals

Serving your direct reports through accountability and short-range goals is important. Ask them, "What progress have you made on your quarterly milestones?"[19] How can you serve someone if you don't know where they are?

Note: This step is optional and can be eliminated if quarterly goals are reviewed in another meeting. For example, I do quarterly goal check-ins in a biweekly management meeting instead of one-on-ones.

4 Step Four: Report on Last Week's To-Dos

Written to-dos increase clarity, accountability, and motivation to act and complete tasks on time. Keep in mind that one-on-ones may not be the only place where reports provide accountability. And since some one-on-ones may not include tasks and projects, to-dos may not be relevant for every meeting. This step can be as simple and fast as the report saying, "Everything's finished." If previous to-dos have not been completed, discuss why. Sometimes people need help or encouragement to complete a to-do.

Note: This step is optional and can be eliminated if weekly to-dos are tracked elsewhere.

5 Step Five: Prioritize and Talk Through Discussion Points

What issues should you discuss? Every one-on-one should include discussion points or topics of interest to your direct report. These should be generated prior to the meeting and the manager should review the list and add to it, if desired. At the same time, these meetings have an informal tone and some of the best discussion items pop up during dialogue. Keep this meeting flexible and adaptable while prioritizing key points of discussion. If a big issue surfaces, adjust the time allotted or schedule an additional one-on-one to dedicate the time needed to discuss or resolve it.

Here are additional ideas for discussion points:

- Discuss something relevant to their work that week. This is the most common topic.
- Give praise. For example, you could point out where you saw them demonstrate company values and culture.
- Offer constructive criticism. People become guarded and defensive when they feel they are about to be judged or criticized. Begin with a compliment or some affirmation, and

they are likely to lower their guard. When you start with something positive, people aren't as likely to feel under attack.

- Provide coaching on any new policies and procedures. Give them a chance to ask questions and voice concerns.
- Talk about the "soft stuff." Get a feel for their emotions and search for evidence of frustration or underperformance. People are seldom candid with their superiors due to a fear of repercussion, especially if they've come from another business where open communication was discouraged. Don't wait until the molehill has become a mountain to address problems of anxiety or frustration.
- Occasionally, inquire about personal development and goals.
- Clarify job descriptions.
- Brief them on upcoming announcements if there is a good reason to inform them personally before you make the group announcement.

A meaningful conversation is a two-way street, but make sure to lead with a listening ear. I call this a *listening posture*, where you're prepared to receive rather than dictate. Don't be a jabberjaw. Make sure your direct report is talking more than you are. Too many leaders don't listen well, and their employees, out of politeness, don't speak so as not to interrupt. Ask good questions to get the other person talking, but then allow the individual to speak. As Solomon states in the book of Proverbs, "If one gives an answer before he hears, it is his folly and shame" (Proverbs 18:13).

Be careful not to control the content of the meeting with asking questions. Use open-ended questions to facilitate dialogue like, "What problems are blocking your progress?"[20] Asking this is key to helping your people move forward. As their direct superior, you have the most power to help remove obstacles in their path. Be open to answers that indicate you are the problem.

Ask, "What decisions do you need me to make?"[21] It's unfortunate when a direct report's work is impeded because of a lack of decision-making on your part. If they know you'll ask this question every week, they can collect these above-their-pay-grade decisions and bring them to the meeting. This decision-making power as a serving leader is so important because you're often the only one supporting them with decisions.

Remember that your foremost goal as a serving leader is getting to know your people. Make it clear that your primary focus is their interest and concerns and that they should come to the meeting prepared to share. One-on-one meetings ideally become the perfect safe place to talk candidly and vulnerably. Galen from Seven Oaks says, "When you start doing one-on-ones, it takes about six sessions to get some meat. The first five sessions are generally light, and it takes time to build trust and learn how to have deeper conversations."

Some reports come in with a list of things to discuss. Others are a little more reserved and need to be coaxed into discussion. If you're open about personal things beyond work, your report will be more likely to open up as well. Discuss their hobbies and dreams. Have regular conversations about their family and get to know their children's names. Give them an open door to talk about their spiritual lives, especially the intersection between spiritual and work life. Listen and learn about the things close to their hearts.

An employee at Seven Oaks recalled that with Dave, one of the owners, "for several weeks, he spent most of the one-on-one time helping me and my husband look for a house and understanding the purchasing process."

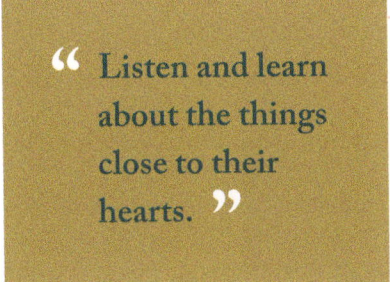

" Listen and learn about the things close to their hearts. "

Consequently, this employee felt she had value beyond the work she could accomplish for the company.

Some reports will feel uncomfortable blending personal and business conversations. Don't force personal connection. If your work culture has not previously fostered a personal interest in people, discuss how you want the culture to change through including a personal element in the one-on-ones. However, you need to earn the trust needed for personal sharing. Go slowly, and let this element of one-on-ones evolve naturally.

> **As a serving leader, you must care about the person beyond their economic value to the company.** ""

Galen admits that sometimes he struggles to know how much to probe. As much as possible, he prefers to allow the meeting to be fluid, with the employee directing and the manager listening. "People want to be heard. They must simply be given the opportunity to do so." Ask open-ended questions that interest them. Again, you want them to open up and not just answer in generalizations.

6 Step Six: Wrap Up the Meeting

Wrapping up a one-on-one meeting is simple and fast because only two people are involved. Review any decisions made along with to-do items, then verify by reading aloud. Next, review any tabled or unfinished items that arose during the meeting. Verify the items can wait till the next scheduled one-on-one, or book a separate meeting to address them. Finish wrapping up the meeting by expressing a highlight you experienced from the meeting.

Following Up after the Meeting

1 Step One: Publish Meeting Notes

The note-taker is responsible to send or post the notes in a place where both parties can review. Regardless of your method, both participants need access to the meeting notes.

2 Step Two: Reflect on the Meeting

Don't be surprised if some of the deepest wisdom comes to you after the meeting. Jot it down and share it next time or send an after-meeting note. This communicates that your care for the direct report extends beyond the meeting. Remember, tabled items can include a parking lot for afterthoughts that you want to bring the next time you meet. I regularly drop items onto the tabled lists that arise between meetings. Then, when preparing for the next meeting, I go to the tabled items to review what's waiting in the parking lot.

3 Step Three: Complete To-Dos

Complete to-dos (if any). This cannot be overemphasized. You shouldn't be too busy to keep your word. If you're overcommitted, think about why that is the case.

This one-on-one interaction goes deeper than work issues. As a serving leader, you must care about the person beyond their economic value to the company.

Jeff came back to Seven Oaks Landscaping during a dark period in his life. For years he had been pursuing the promise of the open road and the fortunes to be made driving truck. But the time away from home took its toll, and he lost his marriage and four children.

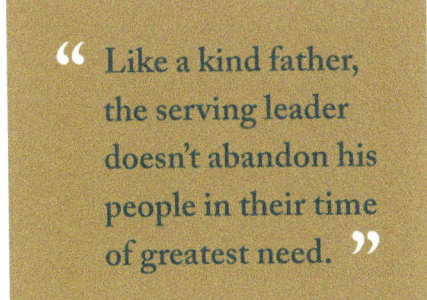

> **Like a kind father, the serving leader doesn't abandon his people in their time of greatest need.**

"When Jeff came back to us, everything was broken," Galen recounts. "His marriage, his finances, his confidence, his dreams. There wasn't much to live for." Changing jobs to work for Seven Oaks again meant a significant pay cut. His finances were in such shambles that he could hardly afford to keep a vehicle on the road, much less pay child support. "He came to us because he needed stability that he couldn't find on his own," Galen said. "We knew he needed a lot of help."

Like a kind father, the serving leader doesn't abandon his people in their time of greatest need. When Jeff reached out to Galen, his former boss took him under his wing and worked to guide him to a better future. "These guys knew I was a mess," Jeff said, shaking his head. "I've worked for other companies, and they would never have put up with what I cost this company. Half the time, I couldn't even afford a car to get to work. And some days, my supervisor, Marcelino, spent most of his time talking me off my ledge of suicide. I wouldn't be alive today if Marcelino had not cared for me."

A profit-centered company would have given up on Jeff. But that is not the call of the serving leader. Galen sat down with him in many one-on-ones throughout the years and mentored him through many decisions, like his personal finances, offering advice and guidance.

"Around here, people are more important than paychecks," Jeff said, choking up as he recalled the support Seven Oaks gave him in his valley of struggle.

There are various ways to reap the desired outcome of one-on-ones. Not every one-on-one will make a life-and-death difference like it did for Jeff. Your organization will have unique circumstances. Customize and make one-on-one meetings your own, but the bottom line is to achieve consistent rhythm and create a safe space for your team to grow and be their most productive.

Appendix:
The Serving Leader Model

Foundational truths for any Christian running an organization must be based on Scripture. These sit on bedrock, not shifting sand. Principles that emanate from such truths are compelling and effective and stand the test of time. It is because of these beliefs that this guide on leading effective meetings has been undergirded by bedrock truths based on the Bible.

The practical side of effective leadership cannot be separated from God's eternal truth. Leaders with a clear and principled set of beliefs must go through a disciplined process of learning how to live out those truths. Without effective practices, even leaders guided by principles find serving leadership elusive and disappointing.

The following five principles and corresponding twenty practices is a compelling and concise philosophical and practical model of serving leadership. I learned about this model many years ago while studying under leadership expert, speaker, and author Dr. John Stahl-Wert. It transformed my beliefs and mindset about leadership. This model is simple, logical, drawn from the Bible, and has been tested by hundreds of mature Christian leaders worldwide. Previously, I led without a clear model or framework that I could wrap my mind around. Those searching for a comprehensive model on leadership, look no further. The five principles (or *actions* as Stahl-Wert describes in *The Serving Leader*[22]) are broad leadership concepts arranged into an easy-to-learn format.

Each of these five principles has four practices or behaviors, which naturally flow from their corresponding principle. Each practice or behavior is identified by a key action step, followed by a descriptive phrase to further clarify the activity. Stahl-Wert's leadership model* is the foundation upon which *The Serving Leader's Guide to Effective Meetings* was written.

The Vision Principle: Cast Vision and Inspire a Shared Purpose

Run to Great Purpose

The four practices of Vision:

1. **Innovate:** Pioneer solutions for the needs and challenges in the world; innovate approaches that create value.
2. **Discover Purpose:** Crystalize the meaningful difference your business makes in and for the world.
3. **Cast Vision:** Communicate your compelling vision for a better future.
4. **Embed Purpose:** Implement great purpose into every aspect of each person's daily work.

Vision is like a bird, with wings propelling it to the destination. One wing represents where its headed, and the other, why it matters. First, vision looks to the future from a current reality and answers the question: "Where is my organization going?" From your current location as a leader, pinpoint a destination. If you know the starting point and your vision shows where you are heading, then charting a clear direction is possible. A vision locked away in the confines of your mind, however, will never work. You must also cast that vision by clearly communicating it to your people. Everyone in your organization must understand the vision

---

*John Stahl-Wert and I have collaborated together and jointly share this leadership model. Any content of his that has been reprinted in this work has been used by permission from the Center for Serving Leadership.

and how their efforts today will contribute to reaching that destination.

Second, vision has a great purpose. It answers the questions "Why does my organization exist?" and "Why does doing my best truly matter?" Serving leaders "Run to Great Purpose," a higher calling, issued from heaven and received in the heart. It's important that your great purpose resonates as meaningful and fulfilling, bringing joy and passion to your work. If a great purpose stays lofty—for example, "Everything I do is for the glory of God"—it can become disconnected from the mission and the practical everyday work. When leaders carry great purpose in their heart and effectively communicate the direction to the whole team, those leaders are often described as visionary. Visionary leaders inspire a shared purpose and point the way forward for all.

Innovate. To innovate is to create something new and valuable. Vision is innovative, necessitating a pioneering mindset that assesses unmet needs and foresees challenges. It then creates, designs, or builds something to fill the void where nothing exists. Innovative leaders imagine or invent better ways of doing pretty much everything. They thrive in the frontier, tend to be idealistic and endlessly curious, and are rarely satisfied with the way things are.

Too often, innovation is perceived solely as a personality trait. However, the "innovation gene" is in the DNA of every leader. God created the world; His nature is innovative. When leaders express creativity, it reflects the image of God as our Creator. His divine nature within us compels us to bring value to the world through invention. However, leaders must learn to innovate by practicing, and it's often through failure that significant breakthroughs emerge.

In *The Serving Leader Model,* innovating and solving problems are sister practices. While close in kin, innovative leaders don't just troubleshoot existing problems. Innovators detect a void, then envision and birth into existence a new solution or idea relevant to some need. Their innovation often answers the questions that others have lacked the foresight to ask. This is why top innovative leaders are groundbreakers and often considered the world changers of their day.

Discover Purpose. Purpose is the fuel your enterprise runs on. It's often buried inside the heart of the leader, coming from one's life experiences and history. If leaders don't know their meaningful purpose, no one else will discover it for them. The discovery process involves an honest search of your heart before the Lord and oftentimes involves key people in your life. The company's purpose can often be known by its leadership, but erroneously confined within the management team. True purpose must be uncovered and revealed to everyone in the organization; this takes work. Crucial questions to ask in this process are "Why does our organization exist?" and "Why does our mission matter?" The purpose uncovered by these questions must be deeply meaningful. Dig deeply into the whys to unearth what matters most.

Sometimes you'll find your true purpose is on the other side of the pain that points to the reason you're unmotivated and low on energy. Ignoring this pain will block access to the fuel it provides. By contrast, purpose also can be discovered through joy and pleasure, sometimes in peaceful moments. Don't miss the emotional energy that rises from the wellspring of joy, or the clarity of purpose that comes when we are free of conflict!

If purpose is missing, leaders will rarely sustain the effort and the perseverance it takes to make a substantial impact in the world. Once great purpose is crystalized in the heart of the leader, it must find its way to the front line of the organization.

Cast Vision. Leaders must communicate their vision to everyone in a clear and compelling manner capturing three dimensions: current reality, what's next, and what's out in the future. Great vision starts with insight about current circumstances and resources. A vision of the direction the company is headed makes little sense if the view of the present situation is blurred. Leaders must exercise foresight, sensing what's around the bend and pointing towards the horizon.

After gaining clarity, leaders are duty-bound to share what they see. Without leaders showing the envisioned pathway, followers tend to become disoriented and wander aimlessly, uncertain of the trajectory. When the vision is clearly communicated, it becomes a beacon, giving everyone a clear line of sight for the future. For the vision to be realized, it must be conveyed by annual and quarterly plans, further broken down into weekly tasks and projects that drive execution.

Embed Purpose. The why within every leader needs to be universally known and shared throughout the organization. Purpose needs to be embedded in the core and driven out to the edges of the organization. These fingerprints of purpose need to be on each person's daily work, infusing even the mundane aspects with deeper meaning. Unless leaders regularly point to the company's important purpose, workers lose drive and motivation because labor feels meaningless from their perspective. It is imperative that leaders intentionally share examples of the way the ultimate purpose of the organization is connected to what workers produce and accomplish. This is best implemented by regularly sharing stories about how the organization positively affected the lives of its customers and employees. As this shared purpose takes hold of hearts, it produces the sustained motivation and energy needed to go the distance.

Together, these four practices (Innovate, Discover Purpose, Cast Vision, and Embed Purpose) awaken meaning and fulfillment within the people who do the work. When a vocational calling is felt in the heart and a clear vision and purpose is set before them, individuals can embrace their work with joy. Leaders "Run to Great Purpose" when they implement Kingdom purpose into everyday labor. This results in a divine sense of meaning in the workplace, creating hope, conviction, and engagement.

The Values Principle: Model, Instill, and Align Values and Build Trust

Raise the Bar

The four practices of Values:

1. **Espouse Values:** Declare what you stand for; clarify and define values by your behavior.
2. **Humble Yourself:** Model and submit to your values by example; be transparent and repentant when you fall short.
3. **Build Trust:** Reinforce the importance of discerning truth, doing what is right, and keeping your promises.
4. **Empathize:** Discern and respond appropriately to the heartfelt needs and emotions of others.

Values are internal guiding principles formed from core beliefs. The external expression of those values shows up in our attitudes and behaviors, even down to the idiosyncrasies of our personality. What we believe, desire, and are guided by influences how we relate to and interact with the world. As such, values determine the culture of every organization.

Values based on righteous standards "Raise the Bar" above standards based on personal desires. When you have a set of high standards that you are unwilling to compromise, your organization will stand above your competition. This will become obvious to your employees and customers. In contrast, leaders who compromise their values breed a culture of instability in their organization, as attitudes, actions, and relationships shift like wind. In the end, every organization reveals their true values by their choices, behaviors, and outcomes. A lack of values cannot be hidden; people within the company know what is true, as do customers and competitors.

Espouse Values. To espouse a value is to deeply commit to it, not dissimilar to the commitment of marriage. Make your convictions clear within the company, leading the way by personal example. Point out why values matter and highlight behaviors and attitudes so others can understand and replicate. Watch for and openly praise team members who are modeling the values of your organization. A behavior rewarded is a behavior repeated! Encourage others by telling stories about those who help support and shape your business culture by demonstrating values. On the other hand, when negative behaviors and attitudes are tolerated, they erode company values. In such cases, seek first to understand, then humbly and firmly help people turn from their destructive behaviors and feelings.

Humble Yourself. One of the most powerful ways to establish good behaviors in your organization is to discipline yourself to live by them. This becomes a humbling experience as you will certainly stumble while attempting to model your own values. "Humble yourselves, therefore, under God's mighty hand, that he may lift you up in due time" (1 Peter 5:6 NIV). When you are willing to submit to the transformational process, failure can be an invaluable learning tool. Excellent standards always expose weaknesses and shortcomings. This is not an invitation to lower your standards; it's the impetus for transformation and growth—raising the bar. This requires a willingness to be transparent when we fall short, and to repent and own the failure when we hurt others. This humble and contrite position will not only foster restoration and healing, but the lessons learned will lift the company and solidify cultural standards.

Build Trust. Leaders build trust by consistently demonstrating values. It's not honest to espouse a value you fail to live out. This speaks to truthfulness and character. Therefore, the foundation of trust is built on values being adhered to in daily practice. This certainly includes setting realistic expectations for yourself and others. With consistency, people learn to expect that you will fulfill your promises and come to trust what you have to offer. Overstating your abilities or what you can deliver breeds distrust. In contrast, sober

and accurate projections reinforce expectations. Nothing ruins trust faster in an organization than consistently being inconsistent. Be truthful, do what you say, and deliver on what you promise. This takes humility since it's tempting to overpromise and underdeliver, just to secure a position, appearance, or sale. Leaders build trust and demonstrate integrity by adhering to their own espoused values. Only then can you invite others to align with you.

Empathize. God has created people with a desire for connection: to know others and to be known. To empathize is to identify with the feelings, thoughts, and experiences of another. Empathy includes being sensitive to others with an authentic desire to experience the world through their eyes. This heartfelt understanding goes beyond facts, logic, and reason. A listening posture enables one to understand a situation and piece together feelings, wants, and needs. Empathetic leaders win the hearts of their people by connecting with them spiritually and emotionally. This type of connection is considered an important emotional intelligence skill. It's the intuitive quality that enables a leader to both discern and respond appropriately to the expressed and buried emotions of people. While love is broader than this, empathy is similar and akin to other virtues such as kindness, gentleness, and understanding (1 Corinthians 13). When people feel understood and known by leaders at a heart level, it awakens desire and energy.

"The purpose in a man's heart is like deep water, but a man of understanding will draw it out" (Proverbs 20:5 ESV). If serving leaders don't invite people to bring their hearts to the workplace, people will remain guarded, their hidden emotions silently affecting performance. However, when teammates become comfortable being vulnerable and empathetic with one another, as modeled by leadership, people thrive. This workplace culture makes people feel safe to expose weaknesses, skill deficiencies, relational shortcomings, and mistakes. An inviting and comforting environment fosters emotional stability, and freedom to express oneself without the fear of ridicule and judgment can be very healing. Empathy expressed in words is a powerful force that the apostle Paul teaches about. "Let no corrupting talk come out of your mouths, but only such as is good for building up, as fits the occasion, that it may give grace to those who hear" (Ephesians 4:29). Imparting grace to others can liberate their talents, desires, untapped passion, creativity, and imagination. When leaders create space to be vulnerable, people drop the shields of their heart and fear melts away. Vitality comes rushing to the surface and motivation for work explodes.

Together, these four practices (Espouse Values, Humble Yourself, Build Trust, and Empathize) "Raise the Bar" in establishing your internal guiding principles on the bedrock of truth and godly desire. These replace the shifting sand of unprincipled opinions and unbridled passion. People expect truth and emotional connection before they risk investing their most precious assets in your organization: their ideas, creativity, time, emotions, and convictions. When values are clear and abided by, it creates a rich relational environment in which people blossom, gifts thrive, and character develops. With regular reinforcement and coaching, the culture of your organization becomes a dependable, trustworthy environment that allows people to become their very best.

The Mission Principle: Lead Strategically, Achieve Objectives, and Solve Problems

Blaze the Trail

The four practices of Mission:

1. **Strategize:** Clarify success factors and set strategic plans to achieve the mission.
2. **Set Goals:** Identify, prioritize, and commit to clear, challenging goals and monitor progress.

3. **Build Systems:** Multiply people's efforts with efficient systems that produce consistent, quality results.
4. **Solve Problems:** Listen to feedback, identify difficulties, remove obstacles, and resolve problems.

The mission of an organization focuses on the creation and delivery of products and services for its customer base. The mission answers these critical questions: What do we offer? To whom do we offer it? What are we helping them accomplish? How will we produce it and get it into their hands? Each question must take into account the strategy and critical partners (inside and outside the company) necessary to accomplish the mission. This is classically known as strategic leadership. A strategic leader's skills include planning, goal setting, and monitoring achievements—all while caring for the people carrying out the mission. To support the fulfillment of the mission, problems must be solved and systems built.

Serving leaders who have a solid mission "Blaze the Trail" in their industry. They evaluate resources, identify needs or opportunities, and chart the path to achievement. Strategic leaders evaluate their position in the marketplace by differentiating their unique contribution. From your chosen niche come the details that inform the company's long-term and annual goals. Clarify your mission by sharing the value you bring to the marketplace, cutting out what doesn't fit. This clarity clears a direct line of sight towards the desired outcome. Now, with the guesswork and risk minimized, confidence and commitment can deepen as people feel empowered and energized with a well-designed roadmap in hand.

Strategize. To strategize, leaders must consider the lay of the land. This requires them to clearly assess what has happened, is happening, and is about to happen. After taking all known possibilities into account, the strategic leader maneuvers accordingly. Market-informed strategy is vastly different from merely guessing or hoping for what the market needs. You can't force the market to desire what you want to produce. The best serving leaders set out to meet a real need or problem. In discovering what the market wants or needs, you clarify key success factors and how you can deliver what the market is seeking. This is the secret sauce of a strategic mission: identifying the sweet spot between the market's needs and your ability to meet them.

Your strategy should be inspired by your desire to generously serve your customer; it can't be motivated by greed, power, or prestige, such as rushing to the market to win market share. Your customer will buy from you for precise reasons. Those reasons must guide and inform the strategic plan. When the mission is crystal clear, then strategic plans can be made. The success of these plans requires a collaborative process with your team. When key people speak into the planning process, what results is greater insight and increased buy-in. Setting the strategic plan includes long-term strategy, resource evaluation, and goal setting—all taking into consideration the people you're leading to complete the mission.

Set Goals. Setting goals is done by breaking down an overarching strategic plan into smaller blocks of achievable benchmarks. This is done by first identifying and prioritizing the work to be done, then defining the work in a specific and measurable way. Goals can be long-ranged or short-ranged with annual, quarterly, or weekly deadlines. People struggle to commit to vague, undefined markers, but thrive when the way is defined in a step-by-step fashion. Goals need to be relevant to current circumstances, but risky and exciting enough to inspire excellent effort. People rise to the challenge, particularly when commitments can be based on clearly defined goals. Goals must be monitored and time-sensitive in order to measure progress, otherwise people drift and lose focus in the whirlwind of daily activities. For example, monitoring progress towards quarterly goals includes setting weekly to-do lists. These are recorded in meeting notes and followed up in the next meeting. Serve your people by helping them set clear, realistic, and challenging goals. A serving leader not only sets goals but guides the goals to completion.

Build Systems. Most work includes repetitive elements that can be stitched together in sequential processes. Building systems requires leaders to shift their focus from working in their business to working on their business. This advanced leadership mindset shifts leaders from operating as product makers to system builders. This can be painful and often feels unfamiliar to product-oriented leaders. However, many leaders hit the glass ceiling of their leadership capabilities precisely because they never build systems! Building systems remains one of the most powerful ways to leverage and scale a product or streamline a service while maintaining and improving quality. A good system must include processes that improve efficiency, quality, consistency, and speed, and prove duplicatable for any qualified operator.

Great systems make work more enjoyable and efficient, and help people more quickly perform at an expert level. Well-designed systems, automation, and refined processes reduce job complexity and simplify difficult tasks, producing more competent, confident, and secure workers. Advanced systems allow younger and less skilled workers to produce higher quality results, reducing labor costs. This enables them to flourish, increasing their dignity and self-confidence, while reducing the frustration of learning something new. This is only possible if leaders are first willing to do the hard work it takes to design the systems that multiply people's efforts.

Solve Problems. Even with the best strategies, goals, and systems in place, unforeseen problems arise that can hamper your mission. No mission is achieved without serving leaders regularly facing and solving problems, doing so with courage and humility. Consider it a privilege to solve problems, even if it's frustrating or overwhelming. It's to everyone's advantage to face challenges that force change and transformation, instead of sweeping problems under the rug. Serving leaders embrace the discomfort of digging through surface issues to discover the root cause of a problem—even if it implicates them. When solving problems becomes a coveted activity and it's safe to be the source of the problem, people will bring their issues out into the light.

Leaders who truly solve problems are hungry for information about the issue. They listen, gather data, and do on-site research about where the problem exists and with whom. Problem solvers must uncover the facts and interact face-to-face (when possible) with the people closest to the problem. Temptation to fill in knowledge gaps and jump to uninformed solutions is nearly irresistible to the human race. Reaching too quickly for answers invites human error, often fueled by biases, assumptions, and lack of pattern recognition. As the leader, it's your job to remove what stands in the way of a solution, which often includes facilitating the problem-solving conversation—instead of wishing it would just go away on its own. It is imperative that serving leaders take responsibility for their contribution to the problem, along with any others who are at fault.

It's important to recognize that those saddled with shame are more likely to abort the problem-solving initiative. To mitigate that risk, come alongside those who admit fault; help them shoulder the burden by humbly identifying with them. This is how God treats us—inviting us to respond to His grace.

Once a problem is identified and a countermeasure is determined, it's time to test it. The solution must be evaluated for its efficacy. Be on the lookout for problems that look solved on the surface but aren't truly resolved. It's imperative to confirm whether an authentic breakthrough has occurred.

Together, these four practices (Strategize, Set Goals, Build Systems, and Solve Problems) enable an organization to "Blaze the Trail" into their chosen marketplace. People thrive when leaders gather the team to search then map out a strategic path, marked by clear goals, leading to desired outcomes. When problems arise, serving leaders move swiftly to identify, remove, and resolve the roadblocks, redirecting their people back to productivity. This makes for a joyful workforce with your customers as

beneficiaries of better products and services. These practices unify people behind the mission, resulting in a fully engaged workforce.

The Encouragement Principle: Develop People's Strengths, Align Teams, and Encourage the Heart

Build on Strength

The four practices of Encouragement:

1. **Align Strengths:** Identify individual strengths and position people in roles that maximize their talents and passion.
2. **Train:** Equip, teach, and coach people for learning, growth, and course correction.
3. **Synergize Teams:** Foster team participation, support team alignment, and experience team identity.
4. **Encourage:** Encourage hearts with affirmation and nurture authentic vulnerability.

The principle of encouragement is embodied by leaders who invest what it takes in discovering and strengthening people's talents, then placing them on the right team and helping them synergize with other members. Nothing encourages the heart more than feeling accepted, connected, and appreciated. This begins by first getting to know people in their unique personality. There is no better way to optimize production than to help others develop and utilize the passions and talents they've been given. You "Build on Strength" when you affirm people for their God-given gifts. When people are well-trained, and more importantly, aligned on a team, they are well on their way to reaching their full potential.

Align Strengths. One of the keys to encouraging people is to understand their skills, passions, and emerging capacity. Together, these three elements make up a person's strengths. People's strengths are uncovered when working together over time. By placing people in different types of work, a sweet spot will emerge. Watch for the type of work that awakens passion and energizes them. Individuals who are doing what they love may leave work tired, but not drained and exhausted.

Be intentional to look beyond passion. Some people love the work they do but simply don't have the natural talent or skill set to become an expert. When passion and skills are mismatched, production and quality suffer. When both talent and passion are aligned, the result is an ever-increasing capacity! When individuals hit this sweet spot, they can often accomplish the work of two people who are not operating in their strengths. Building a culture that focuses on aligning strengths produces an environment in which people thrive and exceed expectations.

Train. Don't make the mistake of believing that a person operating within their passion and natural talent doesn't need good training. Imagine if a great athlete didn't practice or listen to the coach. Natural skill and great passion can only take a person so far, but training is the work of building high performance. Serving leaders equip, train, and coach people to reach their full potential. If a person is left to learn simply through trial and error, progress is slow. By contrast, training or apprenticing fast-tracks learning. Offering small on-the-job course corrections or coaching tips at the proper time gives people a tremendous opportunity for growth. At the highest level, creating a workplace designed to mentor the whole person demonstrates a significant investment, showing people they are more than a tool or a production unit.

Synergize Teams. Serving leaders draw people together into well-rounded teams, accomplishing far more than the sum of each of its members. A synergized team operates like a human body that consists of many parts all working together. Synergy is created when team members with a diverse set of talents work on the same project, each operating within their aligned strengths and unified because there is a high level of trust. Even high achievers accomplish more within a team, so encourage them to collaborate. To ensure team members are syncing, experiment with changing assignments until it's clear everyone is in their sweet spot. Oftentimes, small teams or departments work best with a tight circle of members who perform with greater focus and fewer distractions. Large, all-inclusive teams can drain energy from members, especially when bureaucracy takes precedent over production. When your team is well-rounded in its strengths, carefully synergized, and empowered to be fully focused with clear goals and priorities, the results are impressive. Not only is there high production value, but a collective identity is felt in the heart, giving rise to unparalleled endurance and inspiration.

Encourage. Encouragement ignites the heart. Openly appreciating someone is like pumping oxygen into a fire. Flattery smothers the fire and quenches motivation, insulting even the most optimistic person. Genuine gratitude, recognition, and praise can strengthen a heart. In the face of failure, encouragement reinforces a message of love, bringing hope in distressing circumstances. Tune in to people's struggles and love them in times of weakness. Encourage positive performance with well-timed compliments. Leaders who demonstrate their love for their people in these ways become a bedrock of encouragement. This frees people to lower their defenses and to express authentic vulnerability.

Together, these four practices (Align Strengths, Train, Synergize Teams, and Encourage) result in people finding their productive role in the workplace as leaders "Build on Strength." In an environment like this, individuals can be free to learn, grow, and train—connecting to a sense of purpose. When they synchronize as teams, they blend their expertise and aligned strengths in an environment of trust and respect. This team synergy provides a taste of the body of Christ united as one and "fruitful in every good work" (Colossians 1:10 NKJV).

As a culture of encouragement flourishes, people connect with one another and whole-hearted relationships develop. Loyalty, staying power, and a sense of identity are the fruit of authentic encouragement.

The Sacrifice Principle: Take Responsibility, Delegate, Execute, and Be Willing to Suffer

Upend the Pyramid

The four practices of Sacrifice:

1. **Administrate:** Organize, prioritize, and build clear guidelines and policies.
2. **Delegate:** Commission others to take on responsibility and be willing to help.
3. **Empower:** Authorize and support others to take charge, then hold them accountable.
4. **Execute:** Demonstrate responsibility and discipline and be willing to suffer to get things done.

Sacrifice is the approach to leadership that places the one in charge in the servant's position at the bottom, lifting and supporting everyone above. Leaders exemplify sacrifice with a willingness to go lower, bearing the burden and responsibility for others, even if it means accepting blame for what someone else has done. This bottom-up approach is not a rejection of authority, but instead respects and shares it to avoid abuse. This upside-down approach to leadership is the defining trademark of a serving leader. "Truly, truly, I say to you, unless a grain of wheat falls into the earth and dies, it remains alone; but if it dies, it bears much fruit" (John 12:24 ESV). It's what Jesus demonstrated on the cross and what He showed when He washed His disciples' feet. It's what Paul describes as humbly counting "others more significant" than yourself

(Philippians 2:3). It should be no mystery why this is called "Upend the Pyramid."

While a strong administrative approach sets the stage for people to thrive, use of delegation empowers leadership throughout your organization. Serving leaders get down into the trenches with others, even if there's a cost. When you help others execute, you will need to lead by example and dive in to assist as necessary. This motivates a dedicated workforce to operate at extreme levels of responsibility. Leaders suffer so others can succeed, sacrifice so others can lead, and go low so others can grow.

Administrate. Solid administration runs a tight ship instead of allowing chaos to exist inside the organization. Leaders administrate by organizing, prioritizing, and building clear guidelines with step-by-step processes clearly laid out. This practice cannot be abdicated, or chaos will ensue, even if a company is young or small. Well-defined policies and best practices foster a beautiful, harmonious workplace environment. This must be done from the position of listening to those affected by your administration, protecting against the common abuses of those holding positions of influence or authority. Efficient administrative oversight must not become bureaucratic, but instead remain nimble and adaptive to change. What typically happens in bureaucracy is that policies are set and cemented in stone, without innovative thinking permitted to reshape as needed. Of course, systems and best practices must be written down, but never chiseled in stone. Great administrative leaders balance the risk of poor execution with making things faster and easier. Good administration is experienced by frontline workers as authentic concern for satisfaction; workers know their needs matter and their voices are heard. This creates space for desired feedback, the type that does not fall on deaf ears.

Delegate. Delegation is the act of passing the mantle of responsibility on to another. It's one thing to take responsibility and quite another to lead others to take it. As your organization grows, delegation is required for success.

People need direction, support, and coaching when given greater responsibilities so they can succeed even with increased difficulty. People will be hesitant to accept more responsibility if they feel failure is inevitable or fear they will not be supported. Worse yet, they will likely reject responsibility if they fear being undercut or solely responsible if things are not successful. Micromanagement and overwhelming people beyond their capacity are two pitfalls for leaders who delegate. Serving leaders must match the delegation of responsibility to the level of the worker's ability. This requires two things: increasing responsibility as capacity grows, and properly assessing and adjusting to the right level of needed support. This process of delegation creates a safety net of support beneath the team member who is stepping into a greater role.

Empower. Empowerment is the granting of all the administrative tools needed to perform a role efficiently and the authority to execute. Common resources people need include supportive systems, financial means, equipment, meeting time, and the authority to make decisions. This goes beyond proper job alignment, training, and encouragement. Once delegation, proper aid, and resources have been provided, serving leaders then oversee follow-through. This involves creating a culture where accountability looks like people giving account of their progress using accountability systems, including written action items or to-dos. This method of giving account must be built into meetings so expectations and performance stay on target. This provides the much-needed support it takes to consistently execute.

Execute. To execute, a leader must take ownership and be accountable to others. Disciplined execution requires getting things done, not just talking about it. This is what is expected of a leader: plan, commit, then execute. The act of getting things done well in a timely manner is the art of execution. It takes inner fortitude, drive, and self-discipline to consistently deliver on expectations and meet goals. Often, this requires suffering, going the extra mile and extending effort far beyond what was originally thought necessary. Serving leaders must not only consistently execute, but they are also responsible to help others get things done. This includes occasionally getting your hands dirty assisting others.

When you fall short, take responsibility. It is of noble character to evaluate a disappointing outcome and respond with "That's on me!" Humble leaders consider constructive criticism and feedback a gift, even when it hurts. It is deserving of high respect to be in a leadership seat, and when the team holds you accountable, receive the criticism and respond. In contrast, too many leaders feel disrespected when countered on a matter. When leaders fail to execute and it becomes known, their ego often gets in the way and they feel threatened. In the end, suffering the loss of ego fosters humility.

Together, these four practices (Administrate, Delegate, Empower, and Execute), when instituted with a sacrificial heart, "Upend the Pyramid." There is no better descriptor of the serving leader than the man who is willing to "lay down his life for his friends" (John 15:13). You've prepared the way, positioned your people, and provided the means to an end. Of equal importance is the willingness to get down in the trenches with people when needed. Serving leaders are vulnerable, accountable, and happy to practice radical ownership. This creates respect between executives and the workforce and breeds extraordinary success in the workplace.

Endnotes

[1] Patrick Lencioni, *The Advantage: Why Organizational Health Trumps Everything Else in Business* (San Francisco: Jossey-Bass, 2012), 173.

[2] Kevin Hoffman, *Meeting Design: For Managers, Makers, and Everyone* (Brooklyn: Two Waves Books, 2018), 5.

[3] Steven Brubaker, "Planning Efficient Meetings" (REACH lecture, Lancaster, PA, 2019).

[4] Michael Hyatt, *No-Fail Meetings: Five Steps to Orchestrate Productive Meetings (and Avoid all the Rest)* (Michael Hyatt & Company, 2018), 22.

[5] Hoffman, *Meeting Design,* 102.

[6] Hoffman, *Meeting Design,* 67.

[7] Hoffman, *Meeting Design,* 34.

[8] Patrick Lencioni, *Death by Meeting: A Leadership Fable* (San Francisco: Jossey-Bass, 2004), 229.

[9] Stephen R. Covey, *The 7 Habits of Highly Effective People* (New York: Simon & Schuster, 1989), 273.

[10] J. Elise Keith, *Where the Action Is: The Meetings That Make or Break Your Organization* (Portland: Second Rise), 197.

[11] Keith, *Where the Action Is,* 203.

[12] Lencioni, *Death by Meeting,* 236.

[13] Leigh Espy, *Bad Meetings Happen to Good People: How to Run Meetings That Are Effective, Focused, and Produce Results* (Memphis, Tennessee: Blue Room Press, 2017), 83.

[14] Keith, *Where the Action Is,* 220.

[15] Keith, *Where the Action Is,* 24.

[16] Mark Horstman, *The Effective Manager* (Hoboken: John Wiley & Sons, Inc, 2016), 38.

[17] Mark Horstman, *The Effective Manager,* 39.

[18] Michael Hyatt and Megan Hyatt Miller, "How to Do One-on-One Meetings," December 24, 2019, in *Lead to Win,* produced by Full Focus, podcast, 37:31, https://mh.fullfocus.co/how-to-do-one-on-one-meetings.

[19] Michael Hyatt and Megan Hyatt Miller, "How to Do One-on-One Meetings."

[20] Michael Hyatt and Megan Hyatt Miller, "How to Do One-on-One Meetings."

[21] Michael Hyatt and Megan Hyatt Miller, "How to Do One-on-One Meetings."

[22] John Stahl-Wert, *The Serving Leader: Five Powerful Actions to Transform Your Team, Business, and Community* (Oakland, CA: Berrett-Koehler Publishers, Inc, 2003).

Glossary

accountability: The state of taking responsibility and giving account of what has been done or not done. Higher levels of accountability require the person with the responsibility to give account instead of the person in charge bearing the task of checking up with the responsible party.

action item: See to-do.

advanced-level meetings: A level of meeting that excels in the five meeting disciplines (structure, facilitation, engagement, synergy, ownership) with a customized system of meetings, differentiating between types of meetings. Advanced-level meetings match the size and complexity of the organization, which is typically twenty-five or more employees.

agenda: An outline designed to include logistics and the order of the meeting with a prioritized and sequenced list of discussion points. More advanced agendas can include timing discussion points, various presenters, reference materials, and a list of previous meeting to-dos.

basic-level meetings: A level of meeting that is simple and held only when needed, in which leaders are mostly unaware of the five meeting disciplines (structure, facilitation, engagement, synergy, ownership). Basic-level meetings are ideal for small companies working in close proximity where communication happens organically, which is typically five employees or fewer.

building-block meetings: Meetings that are singularly focused to explore any size issue with adequate time allocated and the right people handpicked for the purpose of the meeting. This category of meetings includes the following types: problem-solving meetings, understanding meetings, brainstorming meetings, planning meetings, decision-making meetings, progress meetings, action reviews, and workshops.

chairperson: A person who prepares the agenda, opens the meeting, and leads the team through the discussion as the facilitator. This includes facilitating the flow of the meeting, using visual aids and questions, managing contributions, and leading healthy conflict.

culture meeting: A meeting that fosters workplace identity and belonging, creating space for people to share life, exchange ideas, and develop connections around festivity and celebrations.

foundational meetings: Meetings that occur regularly throughout the calendar year, typically attended by the same people, and address the core needs of the organization. This category of meetings includes the following types: annual strategic planning meetings, quarterly leadership meetings, weekly management meetings, daily check-in meetings, one-on-one meetings, and board governance or owner meetings.

getting present: To completely focus the head, heart, and body, free oneself from distraction, and become ready to be present with others through body language and words. This includes expressing delight about being together through eye contact and facial expressions.

ground rules: A code of conduct guiding meeting attitudes and behaviors that has been decided upon by the group and is followed by all. Ground rules embody the stated values of the company, creating the desired meeting culture.

healthy debate: A way of discussing differing perspectives, values, and ideas using skills like listening, organizing, discarding, and building upon others' input while building and strengthening relationships.

intermediate-level meetings: A level of meeting that employs a less formal approach utilizing a learn-as-you-go mindset to meetings while starting to implement some of the five meeting disciplines (structure, facilitation, engagement, synergy, ownership). Intermediate-level meetings typically work with companies having fewer than twenty-five employees.

issue: A problem or concern impeding progress. An issue can also be used synonymously with the term *discussion point*.

key performance indicators (KPIs): Numbers that reflect a measurement of an area of company performance.

lean: A methodology that focuses on eliminating waste and improving efficiency, quality, and utilization of people's talents in the workplace.

leveling up: The process of increasing meeting skills resulting in achieving a higher meeting level. These levels of meeting include basic, intermediate, and advanced.

meeting design: The process of creating structure and facilitation methods for a specific type of meeting.

meeting engagement: The practice of focus, concentration, and elimination of distractions in a meeting. This includes understanding others' perspectives and desires and why they matter through active listening and internal processing.

meeting facilitation: The process of designing and leading a meeting by efficiently moving through the agenda tailoring the most effective approach for each agenda item. This includes achieving meeting goals by guiding meeting flow, using visual aids, engaging participants through questions, managing contributions, and leading healthy debate.

meeting horsepower: An effective amount of strength in your meetings to make things happen using the five meeting disciplines (structure, facilitation, engagement, synergy, ownership).

meeting ownership: The practice of taking responsibility for what happens in a meeting, including evaluation and improvement of meeting skills.

meeting purpose: An explanation of why a group needs to meet to achieve a specific outcome.

meeting structure: The processes and procedures around preparing, leading, and following up after the meeting.

meeting synergy: The practice of synchronizing human energy through wholehearted contribution with engaged hearts and minds in a meeting. This includes sorting and fitting parts together and building on each other's contribution through interpersonal connection and discussion.

on-the-go meeting: Unscheduled, on-demand meetings held outside of the meeting room that are short in nature and held without formal meeting structure.

parking lot: A list of tabled items. See tabled item.

reaching consensus: A way of hearing the pros and cons from those around the table that builds toward an agreement that everyone can live with or support.

relational meetings: Meetings that are characterized by people coming together to enjoy each other, share information, resolve conflict, and learn new skills and procedures. This category of meetings includes the following types: introductions, announcement meetings, mediation meetings, trainings, and culture meetings.

secretary: A person who keeps track of time and takes meeting notes. Note-taking includes the recording of important understandings and decisions, assigned tasks, and tabled items.

tabling: An agreement to defer a discussion or decision to a later time.

tabled item: A discussion or decision agreed upon by the group to be discussed at a later time.

to-do: An assignment in the form of who does what by when.

understanding: A conclusion derived from a discussion that brings clarity to a matter with no direct action warranted. This can include insights around events, schedules, facts, happenings, feelings, or perspectives shared in the meeting.

Acknowledgments

I didn't write this guide without the significant support and input from a long list of people. Much of the help wasn't directly tied to the writing or editing of this guide. Rather, I'm indebted to a multitude of situations and people that shaped my perspectives and gave me the opportunity to be part of meetings or to lead them. In light of this fact, I want to acknowledge a few people from my formative years that shaped and forged my interest in meetings, then recognize those who helped bring this guide to fruition.

When I reflect on my growing up years on the dairy farm, it's the place where I first learned meetings of a very informal and basic sort. My first memory of a sit-down meeting as a boy was watching my dad and his brothers perform their monthly "settling up" meeting. They each owned a farm with adjoining properties. The economic climate in the late 1970s wasn't easy. To survive, they borrowed equipment, parts, and each other's labor, then settled their accounts once a month. It was fascinating to watch them negotiate, discuss the value of their trades with each other, and make win-win decisions.

Over the years I've seen a lot of debate in meetings, but I cherish most the memory of my dad and Uncle Clair debating issues. They had sharp minds and held forth their ideas with the boldness of lions, arguing with the freedom that only brothers have. This shaped my concept of healthy debate. To my dad, Uncle Clair, and Uncle Glen, I want to say thank you.

Let's fast-forward ten years. I was a participant in meetings with Dad and my brothers on the farm. I thought I could be bold with my older brother, like Dad did with his brother Clair. But my boldness had an edge that cut my brother too many times. As a naive meeting participant, I never realized until years later that my brother eventually stopped bringing his full self to the meeting. I had bullied,

argued my point, and fortified my reasons with passion while he slowly retreated. Many a time, I mistakenly thought that we came to a good agreement or conclusion only later to realize that my brother had simply gotten weary of disagreeing with me and agreed in order to keep the peace. It wasn't until twenty years later that I reckoned with the fact that I had alienated and seriously offended my brother due to getting my own way—in meetings. To my brother Lavern, I want to say thank you. You forgave me and taught me that gentleness in conversation and listening are better virtues than passionate speech and boldness.

Let's fast-forward another ten years. One of my first experiences of participating in organizational board meetings was with Faith Builders in the 1990s. John Miller was the chairman and role model for me in those formative years. He took me under his wing as I cut my teeth on formal, nonprofit board meetings. John drew me into conversations and wanted my perspective. I felt accepted by John and affirmed even though I was the youngest board member and completely green in my experience with nonprofit boards. When I became chairman, he mentored me into the role—much needed since I had never held that position before. John offered warm relationship and full engagement in meetings. To John, I want to say thank you.

Let's fast-forward yet another ten years. I found myself struggling to lead a new, fast-growing financial organization: Anabaptist Financial. As the first executive officer of the organization, I was ill-prepared for the challenges that arose in those first five years. The board of directors provided me with a rich, nurturing environment where I could learn and experiment. They were unusual men of character with strong board experience. Ken Burkholder and Dennis Martin were chairman and vice-chairman, respectively, for the first fourteen years of Anabaptist Financial. Together, they demonstrated strong synergy and collaboration. They drew me into this highly collaborative approach to board meetings. Informally and unassumingly, they apprenticed me in preparing for and leading meetings. They treated me like their son. They guided board meetings in which participants were united in heart and mind. They built on one another's ideas while each participant was equally valued and drawn into the meeting discussion without domination or overreaching. These were the meetings where I watched and learned about meeting synergy. Even today, these two men are still key influencers in my life. To Ken and Dennis, I want to say thank you.

I dedicated this guide to my two business partners at AgSalt Processing, but they deserve an acknowledgment as well. If they had not jerked my chain and held me accountable to run better meetings, this guide may have never been written. That story is in the opening chapter, so I won't repeat it here. Suffice it to say, after seriously challenging me to fix our flawed management meetings, Doug and Dalen made it safe and even fun for me to practice, innovate, and experiment with new meeting structure and skills. While long overdue for better meetings, AgSalt became my experimental meeting laboratory. We were a small leadership team, and I owe them my deepest respect for allowing those meetings to be a sandbox of meeting trial and error. They meandered patiently with me down the path of better meetings. I couldn't have asked for better business partners.

Another indispensable group from which I harvested invaluable meeting content are the three businesses represented in this guide: Country Value Woodworks, Pioneer Equipment, and Seven Oaks Landscaping. These three companies invited me into a behind-the-scenes look at the way they conducted meetings so I could include them as stories that brought the principles to life. To my surprise, their stories became a significant source of learning for me. I owe a debt of appreciation and respect to these companies which I will never be able to fully repay. May the Lord reward them for their transparency and gift of stories.

I'd like to acknowledge the group of editors and ghostwriters on this project who were instrumental in helping with the writing and editing of this guide. I didn't approach writing about meetings fully trained and armed to write. I'm not a gifted or natural writer. These people deserve special mention because they stepped up when my weakness was revealed. They couldn't edit in a typical fashion because I needed much more from them. What I needed was a writing apprenticeship. I'm grateful for their extra effort in the form of hundreds of sidebar comments, markups, and rewrites that painfully lifted the content like water locks lifting a boat incrementally to higher levels. This group included Caleb Crider, Daniel Smoker, David Ferris, Donavan Lacy, Jeff Hazim, Louisa Seapy, Mark Gingerich, Maria Stutzman, and Thomas Womack.

This guide is illustrated with icons and illustrations designed to assist in the absorption of the material. Kudos for the artwork, layout, and design goes to Renee Miller from Schlabach Printers. She exceeded our expectations repeatedly and guided us in hundreds of decisions, making the daunting task of determining colors, shapes, and sizing much easier.

There is another group that made a bigger difference than I ever anticipated: the reviewers. Most of these individuals offered their reviews without compensation. Some of them went the second mile, dipping into the role of editing and offering extended commentary. All in all, their contributions triggered a landslide of unanticipated but much needed revisions. Some sections were completely rewritten because of their input. The group of reviewers included Gary Garber, Gary Miller, Glenn Jantzi, Greg Wolf, Josh Coblentz, Kevin Weaver, Leonard Meador, Loren Kauffman, Merle Burkholder, Philip Horst, Rachel Mast, Ray Randolph, and Richard Hoover.

Finally, the group of individuals that deserves the highest honors is my inner circle. Like the human body with its primary hidden organs like brain, heart, and lungs, these individuals behind the scenes provided the infrastructure and backbone for the project. I could never have found the courage, hope, and fortitude without this intimate group. Steve Brubaker, Geryll Zehr, and Dr. John Stahl-Wert are most importantly friends—lifelong friends—not merely business associates. Their commitment to guiding this project gave me the morale and spiritual confidence that only an intimate band of brothers can give. I hope to be on their team for the long haul.

A special mention goes to Dr. John Stahl-Wert. In addition to John's friendship, his leadership training from Center for Serving Leadership has transformed my leadership more than any other leadership book or mentor. His five serving leader principles have been embedded throughout this guide and are explicitly represented in the appendix, *The Serving Leader Model*. I highly recommend his online or in-person training to any leader seeking leadership training. You can access his training resources at https://centerforservingleadership.com.

There is another person in this inner circle: my daughter Maribeth Lacy. As managing editor, she wore more hats than is fair for one person to wear. She was more than a managing editor; she managed everything. Her relentless energy and tenacious commitment to draw out and arrange the content was unparalleled. She suffered with me as I languished in learning to write. She rewrote much of the content to better reflect what I couldn't express through my pen. It's impossible to put a value on her contribution. Thank you, Maribeth.

Last but not least is the most intimate person inside my inner circle: my wife Amy. While supportive of this project, neither of us realized the amount of energy, focus, and time this guide would require of and cost us. She stood with me like a true companion, comforting, loving and yes, waiting for me to be done with this project.

Business Biographies

Country Value Woodworks is an Amish-owned furniture manu-facturing business specializing in solid hardwood home furniture. Founded by Elam Esh in 1990, the company is located in Quarryville, Pennsylvania, with forty-five employees. The company has expanded its distribution network across the United States and specialized its manu-facturing with Lean methodology, which has allowed them to efficiently offer the coveted service of customization on all their products.

Pioneer Equipment is an Amish-owned original equipment manu-facturer (OEM) in the metal fabrication industry. The company was founded by Wayne Wengerd in 1978 and is located in Dalton, Ohio. Currently his seven sons and one daughter own and operate the busi-ness. They employ third-generation family members along with forty other dedicated employees. The business started with building horse-drawn farm equipment and has since added Pioneer Carriage, Custom Fabrication, and Flextur™. Flextur™ products bring Lean workflow solutions to the industrial market. For more information, visit https://pioneerfarmequipment.com.

Seven Oaks Landscapes-Hardscapes Inc. is a business that specializes in outdoor living spaces and provides installation and maintenance services. Founded by German Baptist David Bower in 1991, the company is located in Glade Hill, Virginia, and has grown into a partnership of four individuals. They have over sixty employees, many of whom have been with the company for over ten years.

AgSalt Processing is a manufacturer of premium ice melt blends, feed mixing products, bulk rock and solar salt, and other quality products. Founded by Merle Herr in 1990, the company is located in Gettysburg, Pennsylvania, and staffed with twenty employees, many of whom are related. Their ice melt brand, TruMelt, is unique due to its honest, full-disclosure labeling. For more information, visit http://www.agsalt.com.